THE OXFORD IBSEN

THE VIKINGS AT HELGELAND

PLAY IN FOUR ACTS

Translated by
JAMES WALTER McFARLANE

D1386037

London
OXFORD UNIVERSITY PRESS
NEW YORK   TORONTO
1962

Oxford University Press, Amen House, London, E.C.4

GLASGOW   NEW YORK   TORONTO   MELBOURNE   WELLINGTON
BOMBAY   CALCUTTA   MADRAS   KARACHI   LAHORE   DACCA
CAPE TOWN   SALISBURY   NAIROBI   IBADAN   ACCRA
KUALA LUMPUR   HONG KONG

PRINTED IN GREAT BRITAIN

PUBLISHER'S NOTE

The text of this edition of *The Vikings at Helgeland* is taken from
Volume II (1962), the third volume to be published of The Oxford
Ibsen, a newly translated edition of the plays under the general
editorship of James Walter McFarlane; this volume, which con-
tains also *Love's Comedy* and *The Pretenders*, includes a full intro-
duction, bibliography, early drafts of the plays, and notes on dates
of composition and contemporary reception.

1962

CHARACTERS

ÖRNULF OF THE FJORDS, an Icelandic chieftain

SIGURD THE STRONG, a Viking

GUNNAR, a rich yeoman of Helgeland

THOROLF, Örnulf's youngest son

DAGNY, Örnulf's daughter

HJÖRDIS, Örnulf's foster-daughter

KAARE THE PEASANT, a man of Helgeland

EGIL, Gunnar's four-year-old son

Örnulf's six elder sons

Örnulf's and Sigurd's men

Visitors, serving men and women, outlaws, etc.

The action takes place at the time of Eric Blood-axe, on and near Gunnar's lands in Helgeland in northern Norway

ACT ONE

A rocky coast, which in the background drops steeply away to the sea. Left, a boat-house; right, hills and forest. The masts of two Viking ships can be seen down in the bay; far out to the right, reefs and skerries; the sea is running high; it is winter, with driving snow and wind.

SIGURD *comes up from the ships. He is dressed in a white tunic with a silver belt, a blue cloak, long leggings, fur boots, and a steel helmet; a short sword hangs at his side. Shortly afterwards* ÖRNULF *comes into sight from the hills; he is dressed in a dark lamb-skin tunic, with breastplate and greaves, together with fur boots and woollen stockings; over his shoulders he wears a cloak of brown russet, with the hood drawn down over his helmet and half hiding his face. He is tall and powerfully built, with a long white beard, old and a little bent; he is armed with a round shield, a sword, and a spear.*

SIGURD *is the first to arrive; he looks round, catches sight of the boat-house, goes quickly across to it and tries to break open the door.* ÖRNULF *appears among the rocks; he starts when he sees* SIGURD, *appears to recognize him, and climbs down.*

ÖRNULF [*shouts*]. Stand away, Viking!

SIGURD [*turns, and grasps his sword*]. If I did, it would be the first time ever!

ÖRNULF. You must! And you shall! My men are frozen. I need that shed as a shelter for them tonight.

SIGURD. I need it for an exhausted woman.

ÖRNULF. My men are worth more than your women!

SIGURD. Then they must put a high price on the heads of outlaws here in Helgeland.

ÖRNULF [*raises his spear*]. I'll make you pay dear for those words!

SIGURD [*drawing his sword*]. Then so much the worse for you, you old man!

[ÖRNULF *rushes at him,* SIGURD *defends himself.* DAGNY *and several of* SIGURD's *men come up from the shore.* ÖRNULF's *six sons appear from the rocks, right.* DAGNY, *dressed in a red tunic, a blue cloak and a fur-lined hood, is a little ahead of the others.*]

DAGNY [*shouts down to the ships*]. Up here, all Sigurd's men! My husband is fighting a stranger!

ÖRNULF'S SONS. Help for our father!

[*They clamber down.*]

SIGURD [*to his men*]. Stay where you are! I can deal with him alone!

ÖRNULF [*to his sons*]. Leave me alone to fight! [*He rushes at* SIGURD.] I'll see your blood!

SIGURD. See your own first!

[*He wounds him in the arm, so that the spear falls.*]

ÖRNULF. That was well aimed, Viking!
> Swift is the sword you swing!
> Keen is the blow you strike!
> Even Sigurd the Strong himself
> Would be put by you to shame!

SIGURD [*smiling*]. Then his shame would do him honour!

ÖRNULF'S SONS [*with a cry of wonder*]. Sigurd himself! Sigurd the Strong!

ÖRNULF. But that blow was keener still, the night you stole my daughter Dagny!

[*He throws back his hood.*]

SIGURD AND HIS MEN. Örnulf of the Fjords!

DAGNY [*glad, yet with signs of uneasiness*]. My father! And my brothers!

SIGURD. Get behind me.

ÖRNULF. There is no need. [*He approaches* SIGURD.] I knew you as soon as I saw you. That was why I picked a quarrel. I wanted to test the truth of the rumour that said you were the toughest fighter in Norway. Now let peace be between us!

SIGURD. Nothing better, if that could be.

ÖRNULF. Here is my hand. You are a bonny fighter. Nobody has ever exchanged blows as hard as that with old Örnulf before.

SIGURD [*seizes his outstretched hand*]. Let these be the last ever to pass between us. And with that I invite you to be your own judge in the matter that divides us. Are you willing to state the terms?

ÖRNULF. I am. Now is the time to settle the dispute. [*To the others.*] I want you all to hear now what this matter is about. Five winters ago, Sigurd and Gunnar came as Vikings to Iceland! All that winter they took shelter on my land close by my house. Then Gunnar carried off Hjördis, my foster-daughter, by force and cunning! But you, Sigurd, took my own child, Dagny, and sailed away with her. For this I demand that you pay three hundred pieces of silver, and with that atone for your crime.

SIGURD. This seems to me to be a fair offer. The three hundred pieces shall be paid, and to them I shall add a silken cloak all finely trimmed —it was a gift to me from King Æthelstan of England, and is as fine as any man ever wore in Iceland.

DAGNY. Well said, my brave husband! And thank you, my father! Now at last I am happy in my mind.

[*She presses her father's and her brothers' hands and talks to them in a quiet voice.*]

ÖRNULF. In that case, there can be full and proper reconciliation between us. From now on, Dagny shall enjoy the same honours as if she had been lawfully wedded with her family's consent.

SIGURD. And now you can trust me as you would one of your own kin!

ÖRNULF. I am sure I can. And I mean to test your goodwill at once.

SIGURD. You will find me ready. Tell me what you want.

ÖRNULF. Your advice and help. I have made this journey to Helgeland to find Gunnar. I want to make him pay for stealing Hjördis.

SIGURD [*startled*]. Gunnar!

DAGNY [*similarly*]. And Hjördis! Where are they to be found?

ÖRNULF. At home on Gunnar's lands, I imagine.

SIGURD. And where are they?

ÖRNULF. Almost within striking distance. Did you not know?

SIGURD [*with suppressed emotion*]. Indeed I did not! I have not had much
news of Gunnar since that last time we sailed from Iceland together.
I have been leading a roving life, ranging far and wide and serving
many kings in foreign lands, whilst Gunnar remained at home. At
dawn today we made landfall here, driven by the storm. I knew of
course that Gunnar lived somewhere here up north, but. . . .

DAGNY [*to* ÖRNULF]. And this is what has made you leave home?

ÖRNULF. It is. [*To* SIGURD.] Meeting each other like this is the work of
the gods on high—they must have willed it. If I had wanted to find
you, I would hardly have known where to look.

SIGURD [*thoughtfully*]. True, true! . . . But this affair with Gunnar. . . .
Tell me, Örnulf, do you mean to carry it through to the bitter end,
by fair means or foul?

ÖRNULF. This I must do. Listen, Sigurd, and I will tell you. Last summer
I rode to the Assembly and many men of honour were present there.
When the sitting was over, I was in the hall drinking with the other
men from my district, when the talk turned to the abduction of
women. They taunted me about leaving unavenged all this time the
wrong that had been done me. Then I became angry, and I swore
I would leave for Norway and seek out Gunnar and make him pay
for his crime, and never return to Iceland again until I had succeeded
in my purpose.

SIGURD. Ah, well! In that case, I see you must press hard, if that proves
necessary.

ÖRNULF. This I must. But I shall not be unreasonable, and they tell me
Gunnar is a man of honour. I am also very glad I made the journey.
Time has been weighing heavily on me of late in Iceland. Out on
the blue sea was the place I had grown old and grey, and I felt the
pull to be out there once more before I. . . . My dear wife, Berg-
thora, died a long time ago; every summer my eldest sons went off
on Viking raids; and now that Thorolf was growing up. . . .

DAGNY [*joyfully*]. Is Thorolf with you? Where is he?

ÖRNULF. Out on the ship. [*Points to the background, right.*] There's a fine-looking lad for you! So tall and strong he's grown since you used to be at home. He will make a grand fighter, Sigurd. He is going to be like you.

DAGNY [*smiling*]. I can see it is just as it always was. Thorolf was always closest to your heart.

ÖRNULF. He is the youngest, and like his mother—that's what does it.

SIGURD. But tell me, now . . . this business with Gunnar. . . ? Did you think of going today. . . ?

ÖRNULF. Rather today than tomorrow. I shall be content to accept reasonable compensation. But if Gunnar refuses to make this kind of settlement, then he must take the consequences.

[KAARE THE PEASANT *hurries in from the right. He is dressed in a grey russet jerkin and a deep-crowned hat made of felt. In his hand he is holding a broken stave.*]

KAARE. Well met, Vikings!

ÖRNULF. Vikings are rarely well met.

KAARE. If you are men of honour, then let me take refuge among you. Gunnar's men are after me! They want to kill me!

ÖRNULF. Gunnar!

SIGURD. Then you must have done him some wrong!

KAARE. I only claimed what was my right. We had put our cattle to graze together on an island just off-shore. Gunnar's men took away my best oxen, and one of his men called me a villain. So I took my sword and killed him.

ÖRNULF. Such is within the law.

KAARE. But then this morning his men came and attacked me. By good luck I was warned in time and got away. But my enemies are on my track, and I can expect short shrift from them.

SIGURD. I don't believe all this! In the past I knew Gunnar as well as I know myself. And one thing I do know: he would never do any harm to any man of peace.

KAARE. Gunnar had nothing to do with it. He is away, in the south. No, it was Hjördis, his wife. . . .

DAGNY. Hjördis!

ÖRNULF [*mutters*]. Yes, this sounds like her!

KAARE. I offered to pay Gunnar compensation for his man. And this he was willing to take, but then Hjördis came along and taunted her husband with mocking words and prevented a settlement. Then Gunnar left for the south, and this morning. . . .

SIGURD [*looks left*]. I see travellers there, making northwards. Is that not. . . ?

KAARE. It is Gunnar himself!

ÖRNULF. Take heart. I think I can make peace between you.

[GUNNAR *enters from the left with some of his men. He is dressed in his everyday clothes, brown tunic, long leggings, a blue cloak, and a broad hat. He is armed only with a small axe.*]

GUNNAR [*stops in astonishment and uncertainty at the sight of this group of men*]. Örnulf of the Fjords! Yes, in truth . . . !

ÖRNULF. You see aright.

GUNNAR [*approaching*]. Well then, welcome to my land—so long as you come in peace.

ÖRNULF. If you think as I do, there need be no quarrel.

SIGURD [*approaching*]. Well met, Gunnar!

GUNNAR [*joyfully*]. Sigurd . . . my brother-in-arms! [*Shakes his hand.*] With you here, I know for sure that Örnulf comes in peace. [*To* ÖRNULF.] Give me your hand! It is not difficult to guess what brings you here up north—it is Hjördis, your foster-daughter.

ÖRNULF. It is as you say. You did me great wrong when you left Iceland with her without seeking my consent.

GUNNAR. You have every right on your side. The damage of youth must be mended in manhood. I have long been expecting you, Örnulf, on this account. And if you will let me make amends, we can soon be friends again.

SIGURD. I think so, too. Örnulf will be reasonable.

GUNNAR [*warmly*]. You will need to be. If you value her as she deserves, not even all my worldly goods would suffice!

ÖRNULF. I shall be guided by our laws and customs, on this you may rely. But now there is another matter. [*He points to* KAARE.] You see this man here?

GUNNAR. Kaare! [*To* ÖRNULF]. You know we are at daggers drawn?

ÖRNULF. Your men stole his cattle. And theft must be paid for.

GUNNAR. Killing, too. He killed one of my men.

KAARE. Because he insulted me.

GUNNAR. I have offered to negotiate.

KAARE. But Hjördis did not want that. And this morning, while you were away, she attacked me and tried to have me killed.

GUNNAR [*angrily*]. Is this true what you say? Did she . . . ?

KAARE. Every word is true.

ÖRNULF. That was why this man asked for my help. And this he shall certainly have.

GUNNAR [*after a moment's thought*]. You have dealt honourably with me, Örnulf. So it is only fair that I give way to you now. Listen, Kaare! I am ready to let the killing of my man and the injury done to you balance each other out.

KAARE [*gives* GUNNAR *his hand*]. The terms are good. I accept.

ÖRNULF. And he will be safe from attack by you or your people?

GUNNAR. Safe, at home and anywhere else he might be.

SIGURD [*points out to the right*]. Look there!

GUNNAR [*displeased*]. It is Hjördis!

ÖRNULF. With armed men!

KAARE. She is looking for me!

[HJÖRDIS, *with a group of men. She is dressed in black, in a tunic, cloak, and hood. The men are armed with swords and axes. She herself is carrying a light spear in her hand.*]

HJÖRDIS [*stops as she enters*]. We meet here in force, it seems.

DAGNY [*hurrying towards her*]. Greetings, Hjördis!

HJÖRDIS [*coldly*]. Thank you. I'd already heard you weren't far away. [*She approaches, and looks sharply at the assembled company.*] Gunnar and . . . my enemy, Kaare. . . . Örnulf and his sons; and. . . . [*She catches sight of* SIGURD, *starts back almost imperceptibly, is silent for a moment, then composes herself.*] I see many here whom I can claim to know . . . but what I do not know is, who is best disposed towards me?

ÖRNULF. We are all well disposed towards you.

HJÖRDIS. In which case, you will not refuse to hand Kaare over to my husband.

ÖRNULF. That is not necessary.

GUNNAR. We have settled our differences peaceably.

HJÖRDIS [*with suppressed scorn*]. Settled? Ah yes, I know you are a clever man, Gunnar! Kaare fell in with powerful friends, and I can see you thought the safest thing was to. . . .

GUNNAR. There's little use your trying to taunt me! [*Evenly.*] We have no quarrel with Kaare.

HJÖRDIS [*controlling herself*]. Very well. If you have settled the quarrel, your promise must be kept.

GUNNAR [*firmly, but without anger*]. It must! And it shall!

ÖRNULF [*to* HJÖRDIS]. And we had half agreed on yet another settlement before you came.

HJÖRDIS [*sharply*]. Between you and Gunnar?

ÖRNULF [*nods*]. Concerning you.

HJÖRDIS. I can easily guess what it was about. But I will tell you this, my foster-father: never will it be said that Gunnar let himself be frightened into anything just because you came with armed men to this place. If you had made your way alone to our house, the dispute might have been settled more easily.

GUNNAR. Örnulf and his sons came in peace.

HJÖRDIS. That may be. But it will sound differently in other people's mouths. You weren't so sure of peace yourself yesterday, Gunnar, when you sent our son Egil to the south as soon as the news arrived that Örnulf and his fighting ships were lying in the fjord.

SIGURD [*to* GUNNAR]. You sent your son to the south?

HJÖRDIS. Yes, so he could be safe if Örnulf attacked us!

ÖRNULF. This is not a thing for scorn, Hjördis. What Gunnar did might turn out a very wise move, if you should happen to prevent a settlement.

HJÖRDIS. Fate rules our lives. What will be, will be. But I would rather perish than save my life by any cowardly settlement.

DAGNY. Sigurd is making good his offence, and cannot be called a lesser man for that.

HJÖRDIS. Sigurd knows best what his own honour can bear.

SIGURD. I shall never need reminding of that.

HJÖRDIS. Sigurd is a famous warrior. But the boldest deed was Gunnar's when he slew the white bear guarding my door.

GUNNAR [*with an embarrassed look at* SIGURD]. Yes, yes, enough of that!

ÖRNULF. It is true, this is the boldest deed ever done by any man in Iceland, and so. . . .

SIGURD. Well, all the easier for Gunnar to yield without being called afraid.

HJÖRDIS. If these old scores are being paid off, some others must also be mentioned. You remember, Gunnar, the promise you once made!

GUNNAR. That was a bad promise to make. Must you hold me to it?

HJÖRDIS. It must be kept, if you want us to go on living together under the same roof. Listen, Örnulf! If you are going to make people pay for stealing your foster-daughter, then you must also pay for killing Jökul, my father, and taking all he had!

ÖRNULF. Jökul was killed in fair fight, in equal combat. Your kinsmen did me a worse wrong when they sent you to Iceland without telling me who you were, and then got me to adopt you.

HJÖRDIS. That was no wrong. It was an honour to have Jökul's daughter as a foster-child.

ÖRNULF. It brought me plenty of trouble, that I do know.

HJÖRDIS. It will mean worse trouble for you now, if. . . .

ÖRNULF. I didn't come here to bandy words with women! . . . Gunnar, this is my final word. Are you prepared to pay for abducting this woman?

HJÖRDIS [*to* GUNNAR]. Remember what you promised!

GUNNAR [*to* ÖRNULF]. You've heard the promise I made. Now I must. . . .

ÖRNULF [*exasperated*]. That's enough! Nobody is ever going to say that I agreed to pay a penalty for a death suffered in fair fight.

HJÖRDIS [*forcefully*]. Then we defy you all.

ÖRNULF [*with rising anger*]. And who has any right here to claim for Jökul? Where are his kinsmen? Are any of them still alive? Where is his lawful champion?

HJÖRDIS. Gunnar is, on my behalf!

ÖRNULF. Gunnar! Ah, if you were married to him with your foster-father's consent, or if he had made proper amends for running off with you, then he would be the lawful champion, but. . . .

DAGNY [*pleads anxiously*]. Father! father!

SIGURD [*quickly*]. Don't go on!

ÖRNULF [*raising his voice*]. Yes, I shall say it out loud. An abducted woman has no lawful husband!

GUNNAR [*vehemently*]. Örnulf!

HJÖRDIS [*in a wild outburst*]. Insults! Slander! [*Her voice trembling.*] You'll regret this!

ÖRNULF [*continuing*]. An abducted woman is, by law, to be regarded as nothing more than a concubine. If you wish to regain your honour, you must. . . .

HJÖRDIS [*controlling herself*]. No, Örnulf, I know best what is to be done. If I am to be regarded only as Gunnar's concubine—very well, then he must secure his honour by his deeds, win such high honour that my position will carry with it no shame. As for you, Örnulf— beware! This is where our paths divide. But I hereby swear enmity against you and all your kinsmen, whenever and wherever we may meet. You will never feel safe, either for life or limb, nor shall any of the others who . . . [*With an angry look at* KAARE.] As for you, Kaare! Well, Örnulf took your side, and there is peace between us; but I would not advise you to return home just now. The man you killed has many to avenge him, and it could so easily happen that . . . Well, I have warned you of the danger, and you must take the consequences. Come, Gunnar! We must arm ourselves now! One splendid deed was yours in Iceland, but even greater deeds must be done here, if you do not wish your . . . concubine to suffer this shame for herself and you.

GUNNAR. Be sensible, Hjördis! This is most unseemly behaviour!

DAGNY [*pleads*]. Stay, sister . . . stay! I shall speak to my father!

HJÖRDIS [*without listening to her*]. Away! Home! I was never fated to spend my life as some miserable trollop. But if I am to bear this life of shame, bear it for one single day more, then my husband must *do* something—something that will make him famous above all other men!

[*She goes out, right.*]

GUNNAR [*softly*]. Sigurd, promise me one thing! Promise me we'll talk this over before you leave this land.

[*Goes out with his men, right. During the foregoing, the storm has abated. The midday sun can now be seen, like a red disc, low down on the horizon over the sea.*]

ÖRNULF [*threateningly*]. You shall pay dearly for today's work, Hjördis!

DAGNY. Father! father! You don't mean any harm!

ÖRNULF. Let me go! Well, Sigurd, it will take more than compensation now to settle things between Gunnar and me.

SIGURD. What do you mean to do?

ÖRNULF. I don't know. But far and wide they'll tell the tale of the visit Örnulf paid to Gunnar!

SIGURD [*firmly and composed*]. Maybe. But I tell you now, Örnulf, that you shall never bear arms against him, as long as I'm alive!

ÖRNULF. Won't I? And if my mind is made up?

SIGURD. Never! Even if your mind is made up.

ÖRNULF [*angrily*]. Very well! Go and join my enemies! I'm not afraid to face you all!

SIGURD. Listen to me, Örnulf. The day we two fight is something you'll never see. We are solemnly bound in peace. I hold Dagny dearer than either weapons or gold, and never shall I forget that you are her nearest kinsman.

ÖRNULF. This is the gallant Sigurd I expected!

SIGURD. But Gunnar is my blood-brother—we have sworn eternal peace and friendship. Both in peace and in war we have tempted fate together; and he is to me the dearest of all men. Brave though he is, he has no taste for fighting. . . . Well then, you all know me and you also know that I am not afraid to fight. But now I stand here, Örnulf, and beg you to make peace with Gunnar. Please do what I ask in this!

ÖRNULF. I cannot. I shall be the laughing-stock of all men if I return empty-handed to Iceland!

SIGURD. You will not go empty-handed. Down in the bay lie my two long-ships, laden with all the wealth from my Viking raids. Included in it are many precious and royal gifts, chests full of fine weapons, and many other splendid things. Take one of those ships, choose whichever you like best and it shall be yours with everything on board. . . . Let that be compensation for Hjördis, and let Gunnar go his way in peace.

ÖRNULF. My good Sigurd, would you do this for Gunnar!

SIGURD. For a trusted friend, no man can ever do enough.

ÖRNULF. Give half of all you possess!

SIGURD [*urgently*]. Take it all, both my ships, every single thing that is mine, and let me return with you to Iceland as the poorest man in your company. What I give, I can win again. But if you march against Gunnar, I shall never know happiness again. Now, Örnulf, what is your answer?

ÖRNULF [*reflectively*]. Two good long-ships, weapons and other precious things. . . . No man can have too many possessions, but . . . [*Angrily.*] No, no. . . . Hjördis threatened me! I will not! It would be dishonest to take your things!

SIGURD. Listen to me first. . . .

ÖRNULF. No, I say! I must look after my rights myself. Let fate decide!

KAARE [*approaching*]. The advice Sigurd gives is well meant, but I can tell you a better way of getting your rights. Never count on getting any legal satisfaction as long as Hjördis has any say. But you can get your revenge if you care to listen to me.

ÖRNULF. Revenge? What is your advice?

SIGURD. Evil, I can see that!

DAGNY [*to* ÖRNULF]. Don't listen to him!

KAARE. Hjördis has had me outlawed, and she'll try any trick to have me killed. If you promise to protect me afterwards, I shall go to Gunnar's house tonight and burn it down with everybody in it. How does that suit you?

SIGURD. Blackguard!

ÖRNULF [*calmly*]. How does it suit me? Do you know, Kaare, what would suit me more? [*He thunders.*] To cut your nose off, and your ears off, you dirty villain! How little you know me, if you think I would want any part in such a dirty scheme!

KAARE [*recoils*]. If you don't strike at Gunnar, he will strike at you!

ÖRNULF. Then I will meet him with these hands and these weapons.

SIGURD [*to* KAARE]. Now, away with you! Decent men feel ashamed of having had anything to do with you!

KAARE [*as he leaves*]. In that case, I must look out for myself as best I can. But I tell you this: if you are soft with them, you'll regret it. I know Hjördis . . . and I shall find a way of getting at her.

[*He goes down to the sea.*]

DAGNY. He is plotting revenge. He must be stopped, Sigurd!

B

ÖRNULF [*angrily*]. Oh, let him do what he wants. She doesn't deserve any better!

DAGNY. You don't mean that. Don't forget you brought her up.

ÖRNULF. It was a sad moment the day I took her under my roof. Things are beginning to go as Jökul said.

SIGURD. Jökul?

ÖRNULF. Jökul, her father. When I struck the death-blow, he fell flat on his back on the grass, and he looked at me, and said:

> Jökul's kin will bring disaster
> On the house of Jökul's slayer;
> He who seizes Jökul's treasure
> Gets scant joy from his possession.

And when he had said this, he lay silent for a while, and laughed, and then he died.

SIGURD. You need pay little attention to that.

ÖRNULF. Ah, who knows? It is probably true, that story that tells of how Jökul once gave his children the heart of a wolf to eat to make them fierce. No doubt Hjördis got her share—you can see it in her. [*He stops speaking, as he looks out to the right.*] Gunnar! . . . Are we two to meet again!

GUNNAR [*enters*]. Yes, Örnulf! Think what you will of me, but I cannot part from you as your enemy.

ÖRNULF. What do you want?

GUNNAR. To offer you my hand in friendship before you leave. All of you, listen to me! Come home with me and be my guests for as long as you will. There is no lack of accommodation, no shortage of good food; and we shall not speak of our dispute, either today or tomorrow.

SIGURD. But Hjördis . . . ?

GUNNAR. Will do as I say. She changed her mind on the way home and thought the same as me—that we might still settle our differences if you would be our guests.

DAGNY. Yes, yes! We must!

SIGURD [*doubtfully*]. But I don't know if. . . .

DAGNY. Gunnar is your blood-brother, I can hardly believe you would want to refuse him.

GUNNAR [*to* SIGURD]. Everywhere we have gone, you have been my friend. Surely you will not oppose me this time!

DAGNY. And leave this country while Hjördis stays to nurse her hate? . . . No, no, we must not!

GUNNAR. I have done great wrong to Örnulf. I shall never know peace of mind until I have made amends.

SIGURD [*vehemently*]. Anything else I will do for you, Gunnar, but I will not stay here. [*Controls himself.*] I have sworn service to King Æthelstan, and I must leave to join him in England this winter.

DAGNY. But you will still be able to do that!

GUNNAR. Nobody knows what fate has in store. This may be the last time we meet, Sigurd; and you will regret you did not help me in the end.

DAGNY. And it will be long before you ever see me happy again, if you sail away today.

SIGURD [*making a decision*]. Very well, so be it! Have things as you wish, although. . . . Still, it's decided. Here is my hand. I shall stay here as the guest of you and Hjördis.

GUNNAR [*shakes his hand*]. Thank you, Sigurd, I knew you would. . . . And you, Örnulf? You say the same?

ÖRNULF [*gruffly*]. I shall think about it. Hjördis has bitterly insulted me. . . . I don't want to answer today.

GUNNAR. Ah well, old warrior, Sigurd and Dagny will smooth those wrinkles from your brow. I shall go and prepare the feast. Peace be with you, and we meet again in my great hall.

[*He goes out, right.*]

SIGURD [*to himself*]. Hjördis has changed her mind, he said! How little he knows her. Rather I should say she is plotting to. . . . [*Breaks off and turns to the men.*] All of you, follow me to the ships. I want to select some fine gifts for Gunnar and his household.

DAGNY. Pick the best things we have. And you, Father . . . you'll get no peace from me until you give in.

[*She goes with* SIGURD *and the men down towards the sea in the background.*]

ÖRNULF. Give in. Yes, if Gunnar had no women in the house, then. . . . Ah, if only I knew where I could strike her! . . . Is that you, Thorolf?

THOROLF [*enters hastily*]. As you see! Is it true what I hear—you have had a meeting with Gunnar?

ÖRNULF. Yes!

THOROLF. And you quarrelled with him?

ÖRNULF. With Hjördis I did, at least.

THOROLF. Then take heart! Revenge is yours!

ÖRNULF. Revenge? Who avenges me?

THOROLF. Listen. I was standing aboard ship when a man came running by with a stave in his hand, and he shouted: 'If you are one of Örnulf's men, greet him from Kaare, and tell him I am taking revenge for the two of us.' Then he got into a boat and rowed away, and he said: 'There are twenty desperate men out there in the fjord. I'm taking them south, and by tonight Hjördis will have no child to her name.'

ÖRNULF. He said that! Ah, now I understand. Gunnar sent his son away, and he and Kaare are at daggers drawn. . . .

THOROLF. So now he has taken the boat to kill the boy!

ÖRNULF [*taking a quick decision*]. Everybody away! We'll beat him to his victim!

THOROLF. What are you going to do?

ÖRNULF. Leave that to me. I'm going to be the one to take revenge, not Kaare!

THOROLF. I'm going with you!

ÖRNULF. No, you go with Sigurd and your sister to Gunnar's.

THOROLF. Sigurd? Is he here?

ÖRNULF. You can see his long-ships there. We are friends once more.
. . . You will go with him.

THOROLF. To your enemies?

ÖRNULF. Just go to the banquet. Now Hjördis will learn what old
Örnulf is like! But listen, Thorolf! Tell nobody what I am going to
do! Nobody, do you hear!

THOROLF. I promise.

ÖRNULF [*takes his hand and looks at him affectionately*]. Goodbye then,
my bonny lad. Hold yourself well at the banquet, and let me be
proud of the way you behave. Do not speak except when necessary;
but what you do say, let it be as keen as any sword. Be friendly to
all who mean well to you; but if provoked, do not sit silent. Drink
no more than you can take; but do not refuse to drink in modera-
tion, so that they do not think you effeminate.

THOROLF. Rely on me!

ÖRNULF. Then go to the feast at Gunnar's. I shall also come to the feast,
but in a way they least expect. [*Gaily to the others.*] Away now, my
young wolves! Sharpen your fangs . . . now you shall taste blood!

[*He goes out with his older sons, back right.* SIGURD *and* DAGNY, *splen-
didly dressed for the feast, come up from the shore, followed by two men
carrying a chest. The men return at once.*]

THOROLF [*watching his father go*]. There they go, all of them, to fight;
and I cannot go with them. It's hard, being the youngest. . . .
Dagny, my sister! Greetings!

DAGNY. Thorolf! By the powers . . . how you have grown!

THOROLF. Well, I should hope so . . . in five years.

DAGNY. How true!

SIGURD [*offers his hand*]. Örnulf has a lively lad in you, unless I'm very
much mistaken.

THOROLF. If only he would give me the chance. . . .

DAGNY [*smiling*]. He spares you more than you want to be spared? I
well remember he is almost too fond of you.

SIGURD. Where did he go?

THOROLF. Down to the ship. . . . Let us go now, he is coming later.

SIGURD. I am waiting for my men. They are mooring the ships and landing stores.

THOROLF. I'll lend a hand!

[*He goes down to the sea.*]

SIGURD [*after a moment's reflection*]. Dagny, now that we are alone, I must tell you something that must no longer be kept hidden.

DAGNY [*in surprise*]. What do you mean?

SIGURD. It might well be dangerous, this visit to Gunnar's.

DAGNY. Dangerous? You think Gunnar . . . ?

SIGURD. Gunnar is a brave and decent man. No, no! . . . But it would have been better if I had left this place without this visit to him.

DAGNY. You frighten me! Sigurd, what is it?

SIGURD. Answer me one thing first. The gold bracelet I once gave you. . . . Where is it?

DAGNY [*showing it*]. Here, on my arm. You asked me to wear it.

SIGURD. Throw it into the depths of the sea, so deep it can never be found again. It could mean the doom of many men!

DAGNY. The bracelet!

SIGURD [*in a low voice*]. That night at your father's house, when I took you away. . . . You remember . . . ?

DAGNY. As if I could forget!

SIGURD. It is about *that* I want to speak.

DAGNY [*tense*]. What is it? Tell me!

SIGURD. You know there had been a great feast. You went to your room early, but Hjördis sat on at table, drinking with the men. The cup went steadily round, and many brave vows were taken. I swore I would take a pretty girl with me when I left Iceland. Gunnar swore the same, and passed the cup to Hjördis. She took it, stood up and swore that no man should have her as his wife unless he came to her chamber, killed the white bear that stood by her door, and carried her off in his arms.

DAGNY. Yes, I know!

SIGURD. But everybody thought it was impossible, for the bear was the fiercest of beasts. Nobody but Hjördis could approach it, and it had the strength of twenty men.

DAGNY. But Gunnar did kill it. And that deed made him famous in many lands.

SIGURD [*in a low voice*]. It did . . . but . . *I* did the deed!

DAGNY [*cries out*]. You!

SIGURD. When the men left the great hall, Gunnar called me to his room to talk to him alone. Then he said: 'Hjördis is dearer to me than all other women. I cannot live without her.' So I answered: 'Then go to her chamber; you know the conditions.' But he said: 'When a man is in love, he holds life dear. The outcome is far from certain if I were to attack the bear; and I am afraid to lose my life now, because then I should lose Hjördis too.' A long time we talked it over. What happened in the end was that Gunnar went to prepare his ship for sailing, but I drew my sword, put on Gunnar's armour, and went to the chamber.

DAGNY [*proud and happy*]. So it was you . . . you who killed the bear!

SIGURD. It was I. It was dark in the room, black as a raven's wing. Hjördis thought it was Gunnar sitting by her. . . . She was still flushed from the mead. . . . She drew a bracelet from her arm and gave it to me. . . . *That* one you are wearing now.

DAGNY [*hesitantly*]. And you stayed the night with Hjördis in her room?

SIGURD. My drawn sword lay between us. [*Short pause.*] Before day dawned, I carried Hjördis off to Gunnar's ship. She did not notice our trick, and he sailed away with her. It was then that I went to your room, and found you there among your women. . . . Well, you know what followed then. I left Iceland with a pretty girl, as I had vowed. And ever since you have followed me faithfully wherever I went.

DAGNY [*moved*]. My brave husband! It was *you* who performed the great deed! . . . Oh, I might have known! Nobody could have done it but you! You could have had Hjördis . . . proud and splendid Hjördis . . . yet you chose me! I would love you ten times as much, if I didn't already love you as much as ever I could!

SIGURD. Dagny, my dear wife, now you know everything . . . that needs to be known. I had to warn you. As for the bracelet . . . you must never let Hjördis see it! Please do what I ask, and throw it away . . . to the very bottom of the sea.

DAGNY. No, Sigurd, I treasure it too much for that. Is it not a gift from you! But you may be sure I shall keep it hidden from all eyes. And I shall never reveal what you have just told me.

[THOROLF *comes from the ships with* SIGURD'*s men*.]

THOROLF. Everything is ready for going to the banquet.

DAGNY. Come then, Sigurd . . . my brave and noble warrior!

SIGURD. Softly, Dagny . . . softly! It is in *your* hands now whether this visit ends in peace or in bloodshed! [*Briskly to the others*.] Everybody, away now to the feast at Gunnar's!

[*He goes with* DAGNY *to the right; the others follow*.]

ACT TWO

The banquet hall in GUNNAR's *house. The main entrance is at the back; there are smaller doors in the side walls. Downstage, left, is the high seat of honour; facing it, right, a lesser seat of honour. A log fire is burning on a stone hearth in the middle of the floor. In the background, on both sides of the door, are raised platforms for the women of the household. Along the side walls from the two seats of honour, running towards the back of the stage, are two long tables with benches. It is dark outside; the fire lights up the hall.* HJÖRDIS *and* DAGNY *enter from the right.*

DAGNY. No, Hjördis, I cannot understand you. You have shown me round your home and from what I can see, you lack for nothing. Everything you have is fine and splendid. How can you possibly complain like this?

HJÖRDIS. Ah! Put an eagle in a cage and it will bite the bars, no matter whether they are of iron or of gold.

DAGNY. In one thing you are clearly richer than I am. You have Egil, your little boy.

HJÖRDIS. Better to have no child than one born in shame.

DAGNY. Shame?

HJÖRDIS. Don't you remember what your father said? Egil is a bastard . . . those were his words.

DAGNY. He spoke in anger. Why pay attention to that!

HJÖRDIS. Ah yes, but Örnulf was right. Egil is a weakling. You can see by looking at him he is no freeborn child.

DAGNY. Hjördis, how can you . . . !

HJÖRDIS [*paying no heed to her*]. Strange how the shame seeps into the blood, like the venom from a snake-bite. The freeborn sons of men are made of different stuff. I once heard of a queen who took her son and sewed his tunic to his bare flesh, and he didn't bat an eyelash. [*With an evil look.*] Dagny, I'll try that on Egil sometime!

DAGNY [*horrified*]. Hjördis, Hjördis!

HJÖRDIS [*laughing*]. Ha! ha! ha! Did you think I meant it? [*Alters her tone.*] But believe me, or believe me not, I sometimes feel . . . an irresistible desire coming over me to do things like that. It must be in the blood. . . . They say I am one of the Jötun breed. . . . Well, sit down, Dagny. You've travelled far these five long years. Tell me, you must have been a guest in many royal households?

DAGNY. I have. Particularly at the court of Æthelstan in England.

HJÖRDIS. And were received with high honour everywhere? Sat at the best seats at table?

DAGNY. Of course. As Sigurd's wife. . . .

HJÖRDIS. Yes, yes. Sigurd is a man of much fame . . . though Gunnar ranks above him.

DAGNY. Gunnar?

HJÖRDIS. Gunnar did *one* thing that Sigurd didn't dare do. . . . But no matter. . . . Tell me, when Sigurd was on his Viking raids and you were with him . . . when you heard the swords whistle as they cut through the air, when the hot blood stained the decks red . . . didn't you feel an irresistible urge to be fighting alongside the men? Did you never put on armour and snatch up some weapon?

DAGNY. Never! How can you think that! I, a woman?

HJÖRDIS. A woman, a woman . . . ! Ah, nobody knows what a woman is capable of! But one thing you can tell me, Dagny, for surely you must know. When a man holds the woman he loves . . . is it true that her blood turns to fire, that her breast throbs . . . that she swoons with a strange ecstasy?

DAGNY [*blushing*]. Hjördis, how can you . . . !

HJÖRDIS. Tell me . . . !

DAGNY. I feel you must surely have known this.

HJÖRDIS. Yes, once. But only once. The night Gunnar remained with me in my room. He took me in his arms, he crushed me so hard I thought his armour would burst, and then . . . and then . . . !

DAGNY [*cries out*]. What! Sigurd . . . !

HJÖRDIS. Sigurd? Who said Sigurd? I said Gunnar . . . that night he carried me away. . . .

DAGNY [*controls herself*]. Yes, yes, I remember. . . . I know. . . .

HJÖRDIS. That was the only time. Never, never again! I thought I had been bewitched. That Gunnar could hold a woman like that. . . . [*Stops and looks at* DAGNY.] Are you ill? First you look pale, then you look flushed!

DAGNY. No, no, not at all!

HJÖRDIS [*without paying attention to her*]. No, I should have gone sailing off into the joys of battle. That would have been better for me, and . . . perhaps for everybody. That would have been the life! So rich, so full! Aren't you surprised, Dagny, to find me still alive here? Aren't you afraid to be alone with me here in this room, now that it's dark? Don't you get the feeling that I must have been dead all this long time, and that this is a ghost standing here beside you?

DAGNY [*uneasy*]. Come . . . let us go . . . and join the others.

HJÖRDIS [*grasping her by the arm*]. No, stay! Can you understand, Dagny, how anybody can still be alive after having remained here five nights?

DAGNY. Five nights?

HJÖRDIS. Here in the north every night is as long as a winter. [*Quickly and with a changed expression.*] Yet it's quite wonderful in other ways, believe me! You will see sights here, the like of which you've never seen in England's royal courts. While you are my guest, we shall be as close as sisters. We shall go down to the sea when the storms begin again. You'll see the waves racing for the shore like wild, white-maned horses. . . . And then, far out, there are the whales! They charge at each other like warriors in armour! Ah, what fun it would be to sit like a witch on a whale's back, and ride round the ships, and call up the storms, and lure men down to the depths of the sea, singing sweet enchantments!

DAGNY. For shame, Hjördis, how can you say such things!

HJÖRDIS. Can *you* sing such enchantments, Dagny?

DAGNY [*in horror*]. *I?*

HJÖRDIS. I thought surely you must. How was it you managed to ensnare Sigurd?

DAGNY. These are shameful things to say! Let me go!

HJÖRDIS [*holding her back*]. Because I make a joke! No, listen to me! Imagine sitting here in the evening, Dagny, sitting by the window and listening to the banshee wailing in the boat-house. Sitting and waiting and listening to the procession of dead men, passing here on their way to the north, as they must, on their last journey. All the valiant men fallen in battle, all the bold women who refused to live a tame life, like yours and mine. In wind and storm, they rush through the air on their black horses, with a jangle of bells. [*Puts her arms round* DAGNY *and clasps her wildly.*] Ah, Dagny! Think of making the last journey on so splendid a mount!

DAGNY [*tearing herself free*]. Hjördis! Hjördis! Let me go! I will not listen to you!

HJÖRDIS [*laughing*]. You are a poor, weak thing, and easily frightened!

[GUNNAR *enters from the back, with* SIGURD *and* THOROLF.]

GUNNAR. Yes, indeed! For me, things could not be better. I have found you again, Sigurd, my brave brother, honest and faithful as ever. I have Örnulf's son under my roof. And the good old man himself will soon be following, eh?

THOROLF. So he said.

GUNNAR. All that's lacking is to have little Egil at home.

THOROLF. You must be very fond of the lad. You are always talking about him.

GUNNAR. I am. He's my only child. He'll make a fine and generous man.

HJÖRDIS. But no fighter.

GUNNAR. Now, now . . . you mustn't say that.

SIGURD. But sending him away like that. . . .

GUNNAR. If only I hadn't done it! [*In a low voice.*] But *you* know, Sigurd, how a man with a great love sometimes acts like less than a man. [*Aloud.*] I had only a few men about the house, and none of us could be sure of his life when the news came that Örnulf and his long-ships were lying off-shore.

HJÖRDIS. I can think of one thing that should be safeguarded first, before even life.

THOROLF. And that is?

HJÖRDIS. Honour, and one's standing among men.

GUNNAR. Hjördis!

SIGURD. Nobody shall accuse Gunnar of forfeiting his honour by doing what he did.

GUNNAR [*sternly*]. Nobody is going to provoke me against Örnulf's kin!

HJÖRDIS [*smiling*]. H'm! Tell me, Sigurd . . . can your ship sail by any wind?

SIGURD. Yes, when it is cunningly steered.

HJÖRDIS. Good! I shall also steer my ship with cunning, and I shall get where I want to be.

[*She walks to the back of the hall.*]

DAGNY [*uneasy, in a low voice*]. Sigurd, let us get away from here . . . tonight!

SIGURD. It's too late. It was you yourself who. . . .

DAGNY. I was fond of Hjördis then. But now. . . . I have heard her say things it terrifies me to think of.

[SIGURD's MEN *enter from the back, along with other guests, men and women, and men and women servants. There is a short pause in which people greet each other.*]

GUNNAR. Now let us be seated! I am assured by Thorolf that my chief guest, Örnulf of the Fjords, is coming later.

HJÖRDIS [*to the servants*]. Start serving the ale and the mead. Then tongues will be loosened, and men's minds made merry.

[GUNNAR *conducts* SIGURD *to the seat of honour on the right.* DAGNY *takes her seat on* SIGURD's *right hand, and* HJÖRDIS *faces him on the opposite side of the table. In the same way,* THOROLF *is shown to his place on the other table and thus sits facing* GUNNAR, *who sits in the main seat of honour. The others take their seats further back. There is a short pause, in which people drink to each other, and talk quietly to each other across the table.*]

HJÖRDIS. It rarely happens that so many gallant men as we have to-night in this hall sit down together. It might therefore seem a fitting occasion to try the ancient pastime: let each man tell of his exploits, then the whole company decides who is the mightiest.

GUNNAR. It is not a good custom where people are drinking. It often gives rise to quarrelling.

HJÖRDIS. I did not think Gunnar was afraid.

SIGURD. Nobody thinks that. But if we were all to tell what we have done, we would never finish—seeing there are so many of us. Why don't you tell us instead about your voyage to Bjarmeland, Gunnar! It was a splendid feat to journey so far north, and we would very much like to hear about it.

HJÖRDIS. A journey to Bjarmeland is child's play—hardly worth mentioning among men. No, you begin, Sigurd! Unless you want me to think you cannot bear to hear my husband praised! You start! Go on! Name the deed you consider best.

SIGURD. Well, if you compel me, so be it. I can mention the time I was on a Viking raid in Orkney; the enemy attacked us, but we drove them out of their ships, and there I fought single-handed against eight men.

HJÖRDIS. That was well done. But you were fully armed?

SIGURD. Fully armed, with axe, spear, and shield.

HJÖRDIS. Nevertheless it was well done. And now, my husband, you must say which of the things you have done was the bravest.

GUNNAR [*reluctantly*]. I once slew two men who had gone berserk and seized a merchant vessel; and afterwards I sent their captives home and let them take their ship free of ransom. The King of England thought very highly of what I had done, and thanked me and gave me gifts.

HJÖRDIS. Really, Gunnar, you can tell of better things than that!

GUNNAR [*angrily*]. I claim no credit for any other thing. Since I last left Iceland, I have lived in peace as a trader. I shall not say anything more about it!

HJÖRDIS. If you yourself keep your exploits hidden, then your wife must speak up.

GUNNAR. Hjördis! I command you to be silent!

HJÖRDIS. Sigurd fought against eight men, and he was fully armed. Gunnar came to my door in the dark of the night, and he killed the bear that had the strength of twenty men, and yet he had nothing but a short sword in his hand.

GUNNAR [*greatly agitated*]. Woman, not another word!

DAGNY [*in a low voice*]. Sigurd, can you bear to. . . .

SIGURD [*likewise*]. Be still!

HJÖRDIS [*to the others*]. And now, good men . . . who is the bravest, Sigurd or Gunnar?

GUNNAR. Silence!

HJÖRDIS [*raising her voice*]. Speak out! I have the right to ask.

AN OLD MAN [*among the guests*]. If the truth be told, what Gunnar did is a greater thing than any other man has done. Gunnar is the bravest of heroes, and Sigurd is next.

GUNNAR [*glancing across the table*]. Ah, Sigurd! Sigurd! If only you knew . . . !

DAGNY [*in a low voice*]. This is too much—even for a friend!

SIGURD. Be quiet, wife! [*Aloud to the others.*] Yes, Gunnar is indeed the bravest of all men. And this I would hold him to be to my dying day, supposing even he had never done this thing. For I think less of it than the rest of you do.

HJÖRDIS. There speaks envy, Sigurd!

SIGURD [*smiling*]. In that you are greatly mistaken! [*Cordially, to* GUNNAR, *raising his glass to him across the table.*] I salute you, noble Gunnar! Our friendship shall stand firm, no matter who tries to break it.

HJÖRDIS. Nobody is trying to do that, as far as I know.

SIGURD. You say not! I am almost tempted to think you asked us to this feast simply to stir up trouble.

HJÖRDIS. How like you that is, Sigurd! Now you are angry because you are not reckoned to be the best man in the company.

SIGURD. I have always regarded Gunnar more highly than myself.

HJÖRDIS. Ah, well . . . second to Gunnar is also quite good, and . . . [*with a side glance at* THOROLF] . . . if Örnulf had been here, *he* could have taken third place.

THOROLF. In which case your own father, Jökul, would have come pretty low down. Because he had to yield to Örnulf.

[*The following exchanges are conducted on both sides with rising, yet restrained, excitement.*]

HJÖRDIS. You are not to say that! Örnulf is a bard, as we know, and it is whispered that he has given himself credit for deeds greater than he in fact performed.

THOROLF. It will be a sad day for him who whispers it loudly enough for me to hear!

HJÖRDIS [*with a mocking smile*]. Would you avenge it?

THOROLF. I would. And men would speak of it near and far.

HJÖRDIS. Then I raise my cup to the hope that you first get some hair on your chin.

THOROLF. Even a beardless boy is too good to bandy words with women.

HJÖRDIS. But too weak to fight with men. That was why your father left you behind by the fire at home in Iceland, while your brothers went raiding.

THOROLF. Pity he did not keep as close an eye on you. For then you wouldn't have left our country a ravished woman!

GUNNAR *and* SIGURD. Thorolf!

DAGNY [*simultaneously*]. My brother!

HJÖRDIS [*in a low voice, quivering with anger*]. Ha! Wait! Just wait!

THOROLF [*offering* GUNNAR *his hand*]. Don't be angry, Gunnar. They were evil words to spring to my lips. But your wife did provoke me!

DAGNY [*in a low, trembling voice*]. Hjördis, if you ever loved me, please do not stir up strife!

HJÖRDIS [*laughing*]. There must be *some* jokes to go with the drinking, if we are to have any fun at all.

GUNNAR [*who has been talking softly to* THOROLF]. You are a good lad! [*Hands him a sword hanging beside the seat of honour.*] There, Thorolf, there is a fine gift for you. Use it well, and let us be friends.

HJÖRDIS. You shouldn't give your weapons away, Gunnar. People will say you only give away things you have no use for yourself!

THOROLF [*who meanwhile has examined the sword*]. Thank you for this gift, Gunnar. It shall never be used in an unworthy cause.

HJÖRDIS. If you want to keep that promise, you had better not ever lend it to your brothers.

GUNNAR. Hjördis!

HJÖRDIS [*continuing*]. Better not hang it on the wall in your father's house, either. Because there it will hang among the weapons of unworthy men.

THOROLF. True enough, Hjördis. . . . Your father's axe and shield have hung there for many a long year.

HJÖRDIS [*restraining herself*]. Örnulf killing my father . . . is something you never seem to stop talking about. But if rumour does not lie, that deed was not quite so gallant as you think.

THOROLF. What rumour is this you are talking about?

HJÖRDIS [*smiling*]. I dare not say. Because it would make you angry.

THOROLF. Then be silent. . . . That's what I would prefer.

[*Turns his back on her.*]

HJÖRDIS. Well, it might as well be said. Is it true, Thorolf, that before he dared to go out and fight his duel with Jökul, your father sat up for three nights with the witch of Smalserhorn, dressed in woman's clothes and brewing magic charms?

C

[*All rise, commotion among the guests.*]

GUNNAR, SIGURD *and* DAGNY. Hjördis!

THOROLF [*in extreme anger*]. Never has so foul a lie been spoken about Örnulf of the Fjords. You made it up yourself! Only somebody as poisonous as you would be capable of a thing like that! You have accused my father of the worst crime any man could commit! [*Throws the sword away.*] There, Gunnar! There's your gift back! I accept no present in a house where my father is insulted!

GUNNAR. Thorolf, listen!

THOROLF. Let me go! But have a care, both you and Hjördis! Because at this very moment my father has in his power somebody you hold dearest of all!

HJÖRDIS [*starts*]. Your father has . . . !

GUNNAR [*with a cry*]. What do you say!

SIGURD [*vehemently*]. Where is Örnulf?

THOROLF [*with a mocking laugh*]. Gone south! With my brothers!

GUNNAR. South!

HJÖRDIS [*bursts out*]. Gunnar! Örnulf has killed Egil, our son!

GUNNAR. Killed! Egil killed! Then woe to Örnulf and all his line! Thorolf, speak! Is this true?

SIGURD. Gunnar! Gunnar! Listen to me!

GUNNAR. Speak, if you value your life!

THOROLF. You don't frighten me! Wait till my father comes. He will set the mark of shame against Gunnar's house! As for you, Hjördis . . . take what comfort you can from some words I heard today: 'By tonight, Gunnar and his wife will have no child to their name.'

[*He goes out, back.*]

GUNNAR [*in deepest grief*]. Killed! Killed! My little Egil killed!

HJÖRDIS [*wildly*]. And you . . . you let him go! You let Egil, your own son, go unavenged! Every man will despise you, if . . . !

GUNNAR [*quite beside himself*]. A sword! . . . An axe. That's the last time he'll ever open his mouth!

[*He seizes an axe from one of the bystanders and rushes out.*]

SIGURD [*tries to follow him*]. Gunnar! Think what you are doing!

HJÖRDIS [*holding him back*]. Stay! stay! The men will separate them! I know Gunnar!

[*A cry goes up from the group of people crowding near the door.*]

SIGURD *and* DAGNY. What is that?

A VOICE IN THE CROWD. Thorolf has fallen!

SIGURD. Thorolf! Ha, let me go!

DAGNY. My brother! Oh, my brother!

[SIGURD *is about to rush out; at the same moment, the crowd parts and* GUNNAR *enters; he throws the axe down in the doorway.*]

GUNNAR. It is done! Egil is avenged!

SIGURD. Let us hope you have not been too hasty.

GUNNAR. That could be, that could be! But Egil! Egil! My bonny boy!

HJÖRDIS. Now we must arm ourselves, and seek the help of our friends. There are many who will seek to avenge Thorolf.

GUNNAR [*darkly*]. He will be his own worst avenger. He will remain in my mind night and day.

HJÖRDIS. Thorolf got his deserts. Kinsmen must suffer for their kinsmen's deeds.

GUNNAR. That is so. But one thing I know—I was a happier man before this killing.

HJÖRDIS. The night of the killing is always the worst. . . . Things will be all right when that is over. Örnulf took his revenge with despicable cunning. He did not want to attack us openly; instead he pretended that he wanted to be friends and then he attacks our defenceless child. Ha! I saw things much more clearly than any of you. I felt sure Örnulf was an evil, cunning man. I had good reason to try and turn you against him and all his false tribe!

GUNNAR [*fiercely*]. Yes, you had! My vengeance is a poor thing compared with Örnulf's crime. He has lost Thorolf, but he still has six sons left, and I have none . . . none!

A SERVING MAN [*hurries in from the rear*]. Örnulf of the Fjords is coming!

GUNNAR. Örnulf!

HJÖRDIS *and* SEVERAL MEN. To arms! To arms!

DAGNY [*simultaneously*]. My father!

SIGURD [*as though seized by some foreboding*]. Örnulf . . . ! Ha! Gunnar, Gunnar!

GUNNAR [*draws his sword*]. Up, all you men! Vengeance for Egil's death!

[ÖRNULF *enters, with* EGIL *in his arms.*]

GUNNAR [*with a cry*]. Egil!

ÖRNULF. Here is your little Egil again!

ALL [*turning to one another*]. Egil! Egil is alive!

GUNNAR [*lets his sword fall*]. In pity's name! What have I done?

DAGNY. Oh, Thorolf! My brother!

SIGURD. I knew it!

ÖRNULF [*puts* EGIL *down*]. There, Gunnar! Here's your handsome lad!

EGIL. Father! Old Örnulf did not want to hurt me, as you said he did when I left!

ÖRNULF [*to* HJÖRDIS]. Now I have made recompense for your father. Now I feel we can surely be reconciled.

HJÖRDIS [*with suppressed emotion*]. That may be!

GUNNAR [*as if waking up*]. Is this some hideous dream making me mad! You . . . you have brought Egil home!

ÖRNULF. As you see. But I can tell you, he has been very close to death.

GUNNAR. I know.

ÖRNULF. Yet you do not seem very pleased at his return?

GUNNAR. I would have been more pleased if he had come sooner. Tell me everything—tell me what happened.

ÖRNULF. That is soon told. Kaare had evil designs against you. He and a band of others went south after Egil.

GUNNAR. Kaare! [*In a low voice.*] Ah! Now I understand what Thorolf meant!

ÖRNULF. I heard what he intended. Such crimes must not be. I refused to pay for Jökul's death; and I would quite readily have killed you in a duel, Gunnar, if there had been no other way . . . but I knew I had to save your child. So with my sons I went after Kaare.

SIGURD [*in a low voice*]. A hideous thing has happened here!

ÖRNULF. When I caught them up, Egil's guards had already been overpowered. Your son was already at the mercy of your enemies, and they would not have spared him much longer. It was a fierce fight! Rarely have I known such vicious fighting. Kaare and two of his men escaped inland. The others sleep soundly—it will be very hard to wake them.

GUNNAR [*tense*]. But you . . . you, Örnulf?

ÖRNULF [*darkly*]. Six sons followed me into the fight.

GUNNAR [*breathlessly*]. And came back?

ÖRNULF. None.

GUNNAR [*appalled*]. None! [*In a low voice.*] Oh, Thorolf! Thorolf!

[*Great emotion among the crowd.* HJÖRDIS *seems to be fighting an inner battle with herself.* DAGNY *weeps softly by the seat of honour, right.* SIGURD *stands beside her, deeply grieved.*]

ÖRNULF [*after a short pause*]. It is hard, having once flourished like a sturdy tree, then to find the branches stripped off in a single storm. But men must live and men must die. . . . Hand me the cup, and I shall drink to the memory of my sons. [*One of* SIGURD'*s* MEN *brings him a drinking horn.*] Wherever you ride now, my brave sons, I salute you! The great gates of bronze will not shut close on your heels, for you come to the halls of the dead with a mighty following. [*He drinks, and hands back the horn.*] And now home to Iceland. Örnulf's last fight is done. The old tree has only one green branch left, and that must be taken care of. Where is Thorolf!

EGIL [*to his father*]. Yes, show me Thorolf! Örnulf says he will carve me a ship with lots and lots of warriors aboard.

ÖRNULF. Praise be to the powers that Thorolf did not come with us. Because if *he* too had . . . no, strong as I am, that would have been too much to bear. But why doesn't he come? He was always the first to come and meet his father; because we both felt neither of us could live a day without the other.

GUNNAR. Örnulf! Örnulf!

ÖRNULF [*with growing disquiet*]. I see now everybody in the room is standing silent. What has happened? Where is Thorolf?

DAGNY. Sigurd! Sigurd! This is the hardest blow of all!

GUNNAR [*battling with himself*]. Örnulf! . . . No! . . . And yet it cannot be hidden. . . .

ÖRNULF [*vehemently*]. My son! Where is he?

GUNNAR. Thorolf is dead!

ÖRNULF. Dead! Thorolf? Thorolf? Ha! You are lying!

GUNNAR. I would give my heart's blood to see him alive again!

HJÖRDIS [*to* ÖRNULF]. Thorolf was himself to blame for what happened. He hinted darkly that you had gone after Egil and killed him. . . . When last we parted, it was still half in anger; and already once before you had brought death to my family. . . . And besides . . . Thorolf behaved like a foul-mouthed churl at the table; he could not take a joke, and said many evil things. . . . Only then did Gunnar become angry. It was only then he raised his hand against your son. I should say he had good cause to do what he did.

ÖRNULF [*calmly*]. It's clear to see you are a woman. You speak too much. Why? If Thorolf is dead, that is the end of his saga.

EGIL. If Thorolf is dead, I won't get my fighting men.

ÖRNULF. No, Egil. . . . Now we have both lost our fighting men. [*To* HJÖRDIS.] Your father's words were:

> Jökul's kin will bring disaster
> On the house of Jökul's slayer.

You have taken good care to see that his words came true. [*Pauses a moment, then turns to one of the men.*] Where was his death-wound?

THE MAN. Across his brow.

ÖRNULF [*satisfied*]. Ah, an honourable wound. So he did not turn his back. Did he fall to the side, or towards Gunnar's feet?

THE MAN. Half to the side, and half towards Gunnar.

ÖRNULF. The sign of only half revenge. Well, well . . . we shall see!

GUNNAR [*approaches*]. Örnulf, I know too well that nothing I possess can make up for this loss. But ask anything of me you wish. . . .

ÖRNULF [*interrupts him sternly*]. Give me Thorolf's body, and let me go! Where does he lie? [GUNNAR *points silently to the back.* ÖRNULF *goes a few steps, then turns and speaks in a voice of thunder to* SIGURD, DAGNY *and others who prepare to follow him in sympathy.*] Stay here! Do you think Örnulf needs a procession of mourners like some snivelling woman! Stay here, I tell you! . . . I can manage Thorolf alone. [*Quietly and firmly.*] Without sons I go. But nobody shall say he saw me bowed.

[*He walks slowly out.*]

HJÖRDIS [*with forced laughter*]. Well, let him go as he likes. It won't take much to defeat him if he tries coming again to get revenge! Well, Dagny . . . I imagine that's the last time your father will ever set sail from Iceland on a quest like this!

SIGURD [*angry*]. Shame!

DAGNY [*similarly*]. How can you mock him! Mock him! After what has happened here!

HJÖRDIS. Once the deed is done, it is best to accept it! This morning I swore to revenge myself on this hated Örnulf. I could forget his killing Jökul, forget everything . . . except his outrageous insults to me. He called me a concubine. Even if this be true, no shame attaches to it. Because Gunnar is now mightier than your father! He is also greater and more famous than Sigurd, your own husband!

DAGNY [*in a violent temper*]. There you are wrong, Hjördis! . . . And now everybody shall know that you are living under a coward's roof!

SIGURD [*angrily*]. Dagny, what are you doing!

GUNNAR. Coward!

HJÖRDIS [*with mocking laughter*]. You speak nonsense!

DAGNY. It cannot be concealed any longer. I kept silent until you mocked my father and my dead brothers. I kept silent while Örnulf was still here—it was not for him to hear how Thorolf fell by a scoundrel's hand. But now! . . . Give no credit to Gunnar for that famous deed in Iceland, for Gunnar is a coward! The sword that lay drawn between you and your ravisher hangs at my husband's side! . . . And the bracelet you took off your arm, you gave to Sigurd! [*She draws it off and holds it up high.*] Here it is!

HJÖRDIS [*wildly*]. Sigurd!

THE CROWD. Sigurd! Sigurd did it!

HJÖRDIS [*trembling with agitation*]. Him! . . . Gunnar, is this true?

GUNNAR [*with quiet dignity*]. It is all true! All except my being a coward. I am neither a coward nor a scoundrel.

SIGURD [*much moved*]. That you are not, Gunnar! That you have never been! [*To the others.*] Come away, men! Away from here!   ·

DAGNY [*to* HJÖRDIS, *at the door*]. Now who is the greatest man among us—*my* husband, or *yours*?

[*She goes out with* SIGURD *and his men.*]

HJÖRDIS [*to herself*]. Now there is only *one* thing left for me to do, *one* deed to set my mind on: either Sigurd or I must die.

ACT THREE

The hall in GUNNAR's *house. It is day;* HJÖRDIS *is sitting on the bench immediately in front of the lesser seat of honour, busy twisting a bow-string; on the table is a bow and some arrows.*

HJÖRDIS [*stretching the string*]. This one is tough and strong. [*Glances at the arrows.*] And the arrows are sharp and weighted. [*She lets her hands fall in her lap.*] But where is the hand that will . . . ? [*Vehemently.*] To be mocked! Mocked by him . . . by Sigurd! I ought to hate him more than anybody, I see that. But it won't be many days before I . . . [*Brooding.*] Yes, but where is the arm . . . the arm that will do the deed . . . ?

[GUNNAR *comes silently and pensively from the back.*]

HJÖRDIS [*after a short pause*]. How is it with you, husband?

GUNNAR. Bad, Hjördis! All that happened yesterday, I cannot rid myself of it. It lies heavy on my heart.

HJÖRDIS. Do as I do. Find something to occupy yourself with.

GUNNAR. I suppose I must.

[*A pause;* GUNNAR *walks up and down, then notices something and walks across to her.*]

GUNNAR. What are you doing there?

HJÖRDIS [*without looking up*]. Making a bow-string, as you can see.

GUNNAR. A bow-string . . . of your own hair?

HJÖRDIS [*smiling*]. Every hour seems to bring some great deed these days: you killed my foster-brother, and I have made this since dawn.

GUNNAR. Hjördis! Hjördis!

HJÖRDIS [*looks up*]. What is it?

GUNNAR. Where were you during the night?

HJÖRDIS. During the night?

GUNNAR. You were not in the bedroom.

HJÖRDIS. You know that?

GUNNAR. I could not sleep. It gave me bad dreams, all this that . . . that happened to Thorolf. I thought I saw him come. . . . Well, and then I woke. Then I heard the sound of singing, all through the house, strange and beautiful. I got up and peeped through the door. . . . You were sitting in here by the fire. . . . It was burning blue and red. . . . And you were sharpening arrows and singing incantations over them.

HJÖRDIS. There was good need. The breast that must be pierced today is hard.

GUNNAR. I understand. You wish Sigurd killed.

HJÖRDIS. H'm! Perhaps!

GUNNAR. You will never have your wish. I shall remain Sigurd's friend, no matter how much you try to provoke me.

HJÖRDIS. You think so?

GUNNAR. I know it!

HJÖRDIS [*hands him the bow-string*]. Tell me, Gunnar . . . can you undo that knot there?

GUNNAR [*tries*]. No, it is tied too cunningly and too tight.

HJÖRDIS [*getting up*]. The Fates spin webs even more cunning than that. . . . Knots you are even less able to undo!

GUNNAR. The ways of the gods are intricate. . . . We neither of us know what they are.

HJÖRDIS. One thing I know for certain: Sigurd will bring disaster to us both.

[*A pause;* GUNNAR *stands lost in his thoughts.*]

HJÖRDIS [*who has been watching him silently*]. What are you thinking?

GUNNAR. About a dream I had recently. I dreamt I had done this thing you are asking. Sigurd lay dead on the ground. You stood by and looked terribly pale. Then I said: 'Are you happy, now what you wanted is done?' But you laughed and answered: 'I should be happier if you were lying there, Gunnar, in Sigurd's place.'

HJÖRDIS [*with forced laughter*]. Little do you know me, if a silly dream like that can put you off.

GUNNAR. H'm! . . . Tell me, Hjördis, how do you like this room here?

HJÖRDIS. To tell the truth, Gunnar, . . . I sometimes feel too cramped in here.

GUNNAR. Just as I thought. We are one too many.

HJÖRDIS. Perhaps two too many.

GUNNAR [*who has not heard her remark*]. But I shall put that right.

HJÖRDIS [*looks questioningly at him*]. Put it right. Are you thinking of . . .?

GUNNAR. Of fitting out my long-ships and leaving the country. I want to win back my honour—that honour I lost because I loved you above all things.

HJÖRDIS [*pensively*]. You are leaving the country? Well, that might be the best thing for us both.

GUNNAR. The very day we sailed away from Iceland, I saw that things would not go well between us. You are proud and strong. There are times when I'm almost frightened of you. But strangely . . . it's this that makes me love you most. There's a fearful fascination about you. . . . I feel as though you could get me to do anything you wanted, commit any crime, and—no matter what—I would think it well done. [*Quietly, shaking his head.*] Inscrutable are the ways of Fate. Sigurd should have been your husband.

HJÖRDIS [*bursts out*]. Sigurd!

GUNNAR. Yes, Sigurd. You are blinded by hate and thoughts of revenge, otherwise you would esteem him more highly. I should have been like Sigurd; then I might have been able to make life easier for you to bear.

HJÖRDIS [*with deep but suppressed emotion*]. You think *that* is something Sigurd might have done?

GUNNAR. He is a strong personality, and proud, too, like you.

HJÖRDIS [*vehemently*]. If that is so. . . . [*Controls herself.*] No matter! [*Bursts out wildly.*] Gunnar! Kill Sigurd!

GUNNAR. Never!

HJÖRDIS. I was made your wife by cunning and deceit . . . that shall be forgotten! Five joyless years I have sat here. . . . All that shall be forgotten the moment Sigurd is dead!

GUNNAR. He shall suffer no harm at my hands. [*He shrinks back involuntarily.*] Hjördis, Hjördis, do not tempt me!

HJÖRDIS. Then I must find someone else to avenge me. I will not have Sigurd insulting you and me any longer! [*Clenches her hands in a paroxysm of rage.*] With her . . . with that stupid woman . . . perhaps he is sitting with her now, alone, fondling her, and laughing at us. . . . Talking about the way he disgraced me by standing in for you that night. . . . Telling how he laughed at his own cunning as he stood there in the dark, and I didn't know it was he.

GUNNAR. He won't do that! He won't!

HJÖRDIS [*passionately*]. Sigurd and Dagny must die! I shall not be able to breathe properly until those two are gone! [*Comes close to him, her eyes sparkling, and she whispers passionately.*] If you could help me to achieve *that*, Gunnar . . . then I would live with you, and love you. Then I would hold you in my arms in such a warm and wild embrace as you have never even dreamt of!

GUNNAR [*wavering*]. Hjördis! Would you . . . !

HJÖRDIS. Set to work, Gunnar . . . and the gloomy days of the past will be gone. No more, when you come, will I walk from the room; no more will I say cruel things, nor stifle your laughter when you are glad. I shall dress in furs, and in fine silken dresses. If you go raiding for plunder, I shall go with you; if you journey in peace, I shall ride at your side. At feasts I shall sit close by you, and fill your cup, and drink to you and sing sweet songs to gladden your heart!

GUNNAR [*almost won over*]. Is this true? You would . . . !

HJÖRDIS. More than that! Ten times more, believe me! All I want is revenge. Revenge me on Sigurd and Dagny, and I shall. . . . [*Stops as she sees the door opening.*] Dagny! You here!

DAGNY [*from the back*]. Hurry, Gunnar! Tell your men to get their weapons!

GUNNAR. Weapons? What for?

DAGNY. Kaare is coming with a band of outlaws. He means you no good.... Sigurd held him up a short while ago. But who knows...?

GUNNAR [*moved*]. Sigurd did that for me!

DAGNY. Sigurd is indeed a trusty friend to you.

GUNNAR. And we, Hjördis ... we who were thinking of.... Yes, it's as I said.... There's witchery in your talk. Every kind of plan seems so wonderful when you say it.

DAGNY [*astonished*]. What do you mean?

GUNNAR. Nothing! nothing! Thank you for your warning, Dagny. I'm going now to collect my men together. [*He turns to the door, but stops and comes back again.*] Tell me ... how is Örnulf?

DAGNY [*bowing her head*]. Do not ask about him. Yesterday he carried Thorolf's body to the ships. Now he is building a grave mound by the shore.... There his sons are to be buried. [GUNNAR *remains silent and goes out at the back.*] There is no danger before nightfall. [*Comes closer.*] Hjördis, I have one other errand in this house. It is you I have come to see.

HJÖRDIS. Me? After what happened yesterday?

DAGNY. Precisely because of that. Hjördis, you are my foster-sister. Don't hate me. Forget the words that grief and evil spirits put in my mouth. Forgive me all the wrong I did you. Because, believe me, I am now ten times more wretched than you!

HJÖRDIS. Wretched ... you? Sigurd's wife?

DAGNY. All that happened was *my* fault ... the quarrel, Thorolf's death, and all the insulting things that were said about Gunnar and you. I am to blame for it all! Alas ... my life was so happy, but I shall never be happy after today.

HJÖRDIS [*as though seized by a sudden thought*]. But before ...? Those five long years ... all that time you were happy?

DAGNY. Do you doubt it?

HJÖRDIS. H'm! I didn't doubt it yesterday, but....

DAGNY. What do you mean?

HJÖRDIS. Oh, nothing much. Let us talk about something else.

DAGNY. No, no! Hjördis, tell me . . . !

HJÖRDIS. It won't help you greatly. Still, if you wish it. . . . [*With a malevolent look.*] Do you remember once, over in Iceland . . . ? We had been to the Assembly along with your father, Örnulf, and we were sitting with some of the other girls in the council chamber as was the women's custom. Then two strangers came into the room.

DAGNY. Sigurd and Gunnar.

HJÖRDIS. They greeted us politely, and sat down beside us on the bench, and we talked and joked a lot amongst ourselves. There were some who wanted to know why these two young men had come to the country, if it was not to find themselves wives there on the island. Then Sigurd said: 'It's going to be difficult for me to find the woman I can give my thoughts to entirely.' Örnulf laughed, and said there was no lack of highborn women in Iceland, nor of rich ones either. But Sigurd answered: 'A brave man needs a high-spirited wife. The one I choose must not be content to live modestly. No distinction must seem too high for her to aspire to. She must be willing to come with me on our Viking raids, and wear the armour of battle; she must urge me to the fight, and not flinch when sword-blades flash. Because if she is timid in spirit, little honour will be mine.' Isn't it true that is what Sigurd said?

DAGNY [*uncertainly*]. He did, but. . . .

HJÖRDIS. *This* was the kind of woman who could bring joy into his life. And then . . . [*With a smile of contempt.*] . . . then he chose *you*!

DAGNY [*with a start of pain*]. Ah! You mean that . . . ?

HJÖRDIS. No doubt that is why you have shown yourself proud and high-spirited, why you have sought to be honoured by all, so that Sigurd might win honour through you. Is that not so?

DAGNY. No, Hjördis, but. . . .

HJÖRDIS. Surely you have urged him on to heroic deeds, gone along with him wearing the armour of battle, and taken delight in being where the fighting was thickest. Haven't you?

DAGNY [*in great agitation*]. No! no!

HJÖRDIS. Have you then been timid of heart, and thus brought shame to Sigurd?

DAGNY [*overwhelmed*]. Hjördis! Hjördis!

HJÖRDIS [*with a scornful smile*]. Yet all this time your own life was a happy one! . . . Do you think Sigurd can say the same?

DAGNY. Let me be! Alas, you have made me see myself only too clearly!

HJÖRDIS. One word in jest, and at once you start weeping! Think no more about it. Look what I have been doing today. [*She picks up some arrows from the table.*] . . . Feel their sharp points! Don't you think I'm good at sharpening arrows?

DAGNY. And at *using* them, too. Your aim is sure, Hjördis! All this you have just told me . . . I'd never thought about it before. [*With more passion.*] But to say that Sigurd . . . ! To suggest I've been a burden to him, and brought him shame all these years. . . . No, no, it cannot be true!

HJÖRDIS. There, there, you mustn't fret, Dagny! Of course it isn't true. If Sigurd still had the same ideas as he had in the old days, there might be something in it. At that time his only thought was to be the greatest man in the land. . . . Now he is content with a good deal less.

DAGNY. No, Hjördis! Sigurd is still as ambitious as ever he was. I can well see I am not the right wife for him. He has tried to hide it from me. But it shall not go on like this any longer.

HJÖRDIS. What will you do?

DAGNY. I will not be a burden to him. I will no longer stand in his way.

HJÖRDIS. Are you thinking of . . . ?

DAGNY. Quiet! People are coming!

[*A* MAN SERVANT *comes in from the back.*]

SERVANT. Sigurd the Viking is approaching!

HJÖRDIS. Sigurd! Then tell Gunnar to come here.

SERVANT. Gunnar rode off to round up the neighbours, because Kaare was . . .

HJÖRDIS. Yes, yes, I know! Go then! [*The* SERVANT *goes; she speaks to* DAGNY, *who is also about to go.*] Where are you going?

DAGNY. I don't want to meet Sigurd. It seems as though we will have to part, I can see that. But to face him *now* . . . no, no, I cannot!

[*She goes out, left.*]

HJÖRDIS [*watches her go silently*]. And she was the one I was going to. . . . [*She completes the thought by glancing at the bow-string.*] That would have been small revenge. . . . No, this is a shrewder blow! H'm! It is hard to die, but it is sometimes harder still to live.

[SIGURD *enters from the back.*]

HJÖRDIS. You are looking for Gunnar, I suppose. Sit down, he will be here directly.

[*She turns to go.*]

SIGURD. No, stay. It was rather you I was looking for, not him.

HJÖRDIS. Me?

SIGURD. And it is good that I find you alone.

HJÖRDIS. If you have come to insult me, I don't suppose even if the room were full of men and women it would stop you.

SIGURD. Ah yes! I know very well what you must think of me.

HJÖRDIS [*bitterly*]. Perhaps I do wrong! No, no, Sigurd! You have poisoned my whole life! Remember it was you who played that shameful trick. It was you who remained with me in my room, making a mockery of love and laughing slyly to yourself. It was you who slung me over to Gunnar, since I was still good enough for him. . . . And then you sailed away with the woman you loved!

SIGURD. There is much that lies within man's power to do, but the bigger things are decided by Fate. . . . And that is how it has been for us two.

HJÖRDIS. Very true! The cruel Fates rule the world. But their power is small unless they find helpers in our own hearts. Happiness is his who is strong enough to do battle with the Fates. . . . And that is what I am going to do now.

SIGURD. What do you mean?

HJÖRDIS. I shall risk a trial of strength with those . . . those who are over me. But let us talk no more about this. I have much to do today.

[*She sits down at the table.*]

SIGURD [*after a short pause*]. You are making good weapons for Gunnar.

HJÖRDIS [*with a quiet smile*]. Not *for* Gunnar, but *against* you.

SIGURD. That is presumably the same thing.

HJÖRDIS. Oh yes, presumably. Because if I am any match for the Fates, then sooner or later you and Gunnar will. . . . [*She stops, leans back against the table, looks at him with a smile, and continues in a changed voice.*] H'm! Do you know what I sometimes think? I often find delight in painting pleasant pictures in my mind. Then I sit and close my eyes, and think: 'Now Sigurd the Strong is coming to this land. . . . He will burn our house down, and my husband and me in it. All Gunnar's men are slain, and only he and I are left. . . . Outside they set fire to the roof. . . . "One bowshot," says Gunnar, "a single shot can save us". . . . Then the bow-string breaks. . . . "Hjördis, cut off a tress of your hair and make me a bow-string . . . it is a matter of life and death!" . . . But I laugh. . . . "Let it burn, let it burn . . . to me life is not worth a handful of hair." '

SIGURD. There is a strange power in what you say.

[*He approaches her.*]

HJÖRDIS [*looks at him coldly*]. Are you going to sit beside me?

SIGURD. You think I feel bitter towards you? Hjördis, this is the last chance we shall have of talking together. There is something that gnaws at me like a cancer, and I cannot leave you with things as they are. You must know me better.

HJÖRDIS. What do you want?

SIGURD. To tell you a story.

HJÖRDIS. Is it sad?

SIGURD. Sad, as life itself.

HJÖRDIS [*bitterly*]. How do you know life can be sad?

D

SIGURD. That you must decide when my story is finished.

HJÖRDIS. Tell me, then. Meanwhile I shall work.

[*He sits on a low stool on her right.*]

SIGURD. There were once two young men who sailed as Vikings from Norway to win riches and honour. They had sworn each other friendship, and they stood firm by each other wherever they went.

HJÖRDIS. And these two men were called Sigurd and Gunnar?

SIGURD. We can call them that. After some time they came to Iceland, where there was living an old chieftain who had left Norway at the time of King Harald. He had two beautiful women in his house, but one of them, his foster-daughter, was the finest of all, because she was clever and full of spirit. And the two men talked a lot about her, and they both said they had never seen a lovelier woman.

HJÖRDIS [*tense*]. Both? Are you making fun of me?

SIGURD. Gunnar thought about her night and day, and so did Sigurd. But both said nothing. She gave no sign of whether she liked Gunnar; but it was easier to see that she wasn't attracted to Sigurd.

HJÖRDIS [*breathlessly*]. Go on! please!

SIGURD. Yet Sigurd thought about her all the more; but nobody knew of this. One evening it happened that people were sitting round drinking, when this proud woman swore that the only man who should possess her would be he who performed a certain heroic deed, which she named. Sigurd was overjoyed at this, because he felt within him the strength to do that deed. But Gunnar took him aside, and spoke of his love. . . . And Sigurd kept silent about his own, but went and. . . .

HJÖRDIS [*bursts out*]. Sigurd! Sigurd! [*Masters herself.*] And this story— is it true?

SIGURD. It is. One of us had to give way. Gunnar was my friend. I couldn't do anything else. That was how you became Gunnar's wife and I took another woman.

HJÖRDIS. And came to love her?

SIGURD. I came to value her. But there is only *one* woman Sigurd has ever loved, and that was the woman who treated him coldly from the very first day they met. [*He gets up.*] This is the end of my story. Now let us part. To you, Gunnar's wife, I say goodbye. We shall never meet again.

HJÖRDIS [*jumps up*]. No, stay! Alas for us both! Sigurd, what have you done!

SIGURD [*starts*]. Done? What is this?

HJÖRDIS. And all this you tell me now! Yet, no . . . it cannot be true!

SIGURD. This is the last time we shall talk together. Every word is true. . . . I wanted you to think more kindly of me, and that is why I had to speak.

HJÖRDIS [*involuntarily clasps her hands, and quietly looks at him in amazement*]. Loved . . . loved me . . . you! [*Vehemently, as she comes closer to him.*] I don't believe you! [*Looks fixedly at him, and bursts out in wild anguish.*] Yes, it is true . . . and a sad thing for us both.

[*She buries her face in her hands and walks away.*]

SIGURD [*appalled*]. Hjördis!

HJÖRDIS [*quietly, struggling between laughter and tears*]. Don't pay any attention to me! All I meant to say was. . . . [*She places her hand on his arm.*] Sigurd, you have not finished your story. That proud woman you were talking about. . . . She loved you too!

SIGURD [*starts back*]. You!

HJÖRDIS [*with composure*]. Yes, Sigurd! I loved you, I know that now. You say I was silent and cold with you. What else is there for a woman to do? If I had made a show of my love, I would scarcely have been worthy of you. You always seemed to me the finest of all men. And then to see you as the husband of somebody else, that caused me a kind of bitter pain I never properly understood.

SIGURD [*much shaken*]. This is a wretched web the Fates have spun around us.

HJÖRDIS. You have yourself to blame. Men should act with strength and courage. When I imposed that severe test for the man who was to win me, of course I was thinking of you. . . . Yet you could go and . . .!

D*

SIGURD. I knew how sick at heart Gunnar was. I alone could cure him. . . . What choice did I have? Yet, if I had known then what I know now, I can't answer for what I would have done. The power of love is strong.

HJÖRDIS [*quickly*]. Well, Sigurd. . . . A trick of fate has kept us many long years apart. But now the knot is loosed. The years to come will make up for the past.

SIGURD [*shaking his head*]. That can never be. We must part again.

HJÖRDIS. We must not. I love you, and I can say that now without feeling ashamed. Because my love is not a soft thing, like the love of weak women. If I were a man . . . by the powers, my love for you would still be just as strong. Up then, Sigurd! Happiness is worth a bold deed. We can both be free, if we ourselves want to be— and then the game is won.

SIGURD. Free? What do you mean?

HJÖRDIS. What does Dagny mean to you? What could she ever be to you? Nothing more than Gunnar is to me in my secret thoughts. What does it matter if two miserable lives are thrown away!

SIGURD. Hjördis! Hjördis!

HJÖRDIS. Let Gunnar stay here. Let Dagny go back to Iceland with her father. I will follow you, in battle array, wherever you may go. [SIGURD *shows agitation*.] Not as your wife will I go—for I have belonged to another, and the woman still lives who has lain by your side. No, not as your wife, Sigurd, but as a Valkyrie is how I will come—firing your blood to battle and to great deeds, standing by your side as the sword-blows fall, shoulder to shoulder with your fighting men in storm and tempest. And when your funeral song is sung, it shall tell of Sigurd and Hjördis together!

SIGURD. That used to be my fondest dream. Now it is too late. Gunnar and Dagny stand between us, and both with every right to stand where they do. I destroyed my young love for Gunnar's sake—if I am to suffer the pain of that, at least what I did must not be in vain. And then Dagny—leaving her home and her people so trustingly, putting all her faith in me. She must never suspect that every time she took me in her arms I really yearned for Hjördis.

HJÖRDIS. You mean you would let a thing like that be a drag on your life! What is this strength of yours for, then? And this vigour, and all these fine qualities of mind? And do you think I could demean myself by staying on here any longer in Gunnar's house? No, Sigurd, there are many tasks a man like you could turn his hand to here, believe me. Erik is King in Norway—fight him! Many good fighting men would give their loyalty to you. We would go forward with irresistible might, fighting and striving and never resting until you are sitting on the throne of kings.

SIGURD. Hjördis! Hjördis! This was my dream in my wild youth. Let it now be forgotten. . . . Do not tempt me!

HJÖRDIS [*with dignity*]. It is decreed by the Fates that we two must hold together. This cannot be altered. I now see quite clearly what my task in life must be—to make you famous in every land. You have been in my thoughts every day, every hour, I have lived here. I wanted to tear you out of my mind, but I was helpless. Now there is no need, now I know you love me.

SIGURD [*forcing himself to speak distantly*]. If that is so . . . then I say . . . I *have* loved you. Now that is over. . . . I have forgotten those days.

HJÖRDIS. You are lying, Sigurd! If you have loved me once, you can never forget it—this much at least I am worth.

SIGURD [*vehemently*]. I must! And I will!

HJÖRDIS. That may be. But you *cannot!* You want to stop me, but you won't succeed. By tonight, Gunnar and Dagny will know everything.

SIGURD. Ha! You would not do that!

HJÖRDIS. I would!

SIGURD. Then I haven't really known you. I always thought of you as high-minded.

HJÖRDIS. Evil days breed evil thoughts. The confidence you placed in me was too great. I *must* be with you . . . as you go to face the battles of life. Everything is so cramped under Gunnar's roof!

SIGURD [*with emphasis*]. But honour between men is something you have always valued highly. There are good reasons why I might quarrel with Gunnar. Suppose he were to die by my hand . . . would you still tell everything and follow me?

HJÖRDIS [*starts*]. Why do you ask?

SIGURD. Answer me first. What would you do if I killed your husband?

HJÖRDIS [*looks fixedly at him*]. Then I would have to keep silent, and never rest until I knew you were dead.

SIGURD [*with a smile*]. That is well, Hjördis. . . . I knew it.

HJÖRDIS [*hastily*]. But that can never happen!

SIGURD. It *must* happen. You yourself have cast the die, for Gunnar's life and for mine!

[GUNNAR *and some of his men enter from the back.*]

GUNNAR [*to* HJÖRDIS, *darkly*]. You see what comes now from the seed you have sown!

SIGURD [*approaches*]. What is wrong with you?

GUNNAR. Sigurd, is it you! Wrong with me? Nothing that I might not have expected. As soon as Dagny brought the news about Kaare, I got on my horse and rode to ask my neighbours for help.

HJÖRDIS [*tense*]. Well?

GUNNAR. Nowhere could I get a straight answer. They said what I had done to Kaare was scarcely honourable. . . . H'm, they said a lot of other things, too, which I cannot repeat. . . . I have lost my honour. I am accused of doing underhand things. People will not dishonour themselves by taking my part in things.

SIGURD. It will not be thought dishonour for long. Before tonight you will have plenty of men to face Kaare with.

GUNNAR. Sigurd!

HJÖRDIS [*quietly triumphant*]. Ha! I knew it!

SIGURD [*steeling himself*]. But it also means the end of peace between us. Listen to me now, Gunnar: you killed Thorolf, my wife's kinsman, and for this I challenge you to mortal combat tomorrow at sunrise!

[*In great agitation,* HJÖRDIS *takes a step towards* SIGURD, *but masters herself and remains standing motionless during what follows.*]

GUNNAR [*in profound astonishment*]. Mortal combat . . . ! Me! You are joking, Sigurd!

SIGURD. You have been formally challenged. It will mean life or death. One of us must die.

GUNNAR [*bitterly*]. Ha, I understand. You were talking to Hjördis alone when I came in. She has been inciting you again!

SIGURD. Perhaps! [*Half facing* HJÖRDIS.] A high-spirited woman must of course defend her husband's honour. [*To the men in the background.*] You men, go now and tell Gunnar's neighbours that he is meeting me tomorrow in combat. Nobody will call the man a coward who is ready to fight against Sigurd!

[*The men go out at the back.*]

GUNNAR [*crosses quickly to* SIGURD *and presses his hand in great emotion*]. Sigurd, my noble brother, now I understand you! You are risking your life for my honour, just as once before you risked it for my happiness!

SIGURD. Thank your wife! Hers is the greatest part in what I am doing. Tomorrow at sunrise. . . .

GUNNAR. I shall meet you there. [*Tenderly.*] Sigurd, will you accept a good sword from me. It is quite a valuable gift.

SIGURD. Thank you. But let it hang where it is. Nobody knows whether I shall need it tomorrow night.

GUNNAR [*shakes his hand*]. Goodbye, Sigurd!

SIGURD. Goodbye . . . and good luck be with you!

[*They part;* GUNNAR *goes out left,* SIGURD *casts a glance at* HJÖRDIS *and goes out at the back.*]

HJÖRDIS [*after a pause, softly and pensively*]. They fight tomorrow. Which will be killed? [*Is silent for a moment, then cries out as though making a sudden resolve.*] Whoever is killed . . . Sigurd and I shall still be together!

ACT FOUR

By the shore. It is evening; the moon can occasionally be seen through dark and ragged storm-clouds. In the background there is a black, newly-made gravemound.

ÖRNULF *is sitting on a rock, right foreground, his head bare, his elbows propped on his knees, and his face hidden in his hands. His men are digging the gravemound by the light of torches. After a short pause,* SIGURD *and* DAGNY *come out of the boat-house, where a log fire is burning.*

DAGNY [*in a low voice*]. He is still sitting there. [*Holds* SIGURD *back.*] No, don't speak to him!

SIGURD. You are right. It is too soon. Best leave him alone.

DAGNY [*goes over to the right, and looks at her father with silent sorrow*]. He was so brave yesterday when he carried Thorolf's body on his back. He was brave while they were digging the grave. But when they had all been laid to rest, and the earth and stones piled over them . . . then he was seized with grief. He just seemed to founder. [*Dries her tears.*] Tell me, Sigurd, when do you mean to sail home to Iceland?

SIGURD. As soon as the storm drops, and I have finally settled things with Gunnar.

DAGNY. And then you will buy some land and build a home and never go raiding again?

SIGURD. Yes, yes, just as I promised you.

DAGNY. And can I take it Hjördis was lying when she said I wasn't fit to be your wife?

SIGURD. Yes, yes, Dagny! You must believe me.

DAGNY. Then I can be happy again, and I will try to forget all the evil things that have been done here. In the long winter evenings, we will talk to each other about Gunnar and Hjördis, and. . . .

SIGURD. No, Dagny! If you want us to be happy, you must never speak of Hjördis when we are back home in Iceland!

DAGNY [*gently reproachful*]. This is unreasonable, this hatred of her. Sigurd, Sigurd, it isn't like you!

ONE OF THE MEN [*approaching*]. There, the gravemound is finished.

ÖRNULF [*as though waking up*]. Gravemound? Is it . . . ? Ah, yes. . . .

SIGURD. Speak to him now, Dagny!

DAGNY [*approaching*]. Father, it is cold out here. There is a storm blowing up tonight.

ÖRNULF. H'm, don't worry! The mound is firm and well-built. They'll lie snug in there.

DAGNY. Yes, but what about you . . . ?

ÖRNULF. Me? I am not cold.

DAGNY. You have eaten nothing today. Won't you go inside. Supper is ready.

ÖRNULF. Supper can wait, I am not hungry.

DAGNY. But sitting so still here like this . . . it is not good for you, believe me. You aren't used to it.

ÖRNULF. That is true. There is a tightness in my chest. I cannot breathe.

[*He hides his face in his hands. A pause.* DAGNY *sits down beside him.*]

DAGNY. Tomorrow you will be making ready and sailing with us to Iceland?

ÖRNULF [*without looking up*]. What do I want there? No, I want to join my sons.

DAGNY [*sadly*]. Father!

ÖRNULF [*raises his head*]. Go inside, and let me sit. Simply let the storm rage about me for a night or two, and that will do it, I imagine.

SIGURD. You must not think of such things!

ÖRNULF. Are you surprised that I want to rest! My day's work is done; I have buried my sons. [*Vehemently.*] Go away! Leave me!

[*He hides his face again.*]

SIGURD [*softly to* DAGNY *who rises*]. Let him sit a little longer.

DAGNY. No, I must try one other way. . . . I know him. [*To* ÖRNULF.] You say your day's work is done. But it isn't. You have buried your sons. . . . But you are a bard. You are expected to compose something to their memory.

ÖRNULF [*shaking his head*]. Compose? No, no! Yesterday I could have done it; today I am too old.

DAGNY. You *must*. Your sons were all men of honour. They must have their funeral song, and none of their kin can do that but you.

ÖRNULF [*looks inquiringly at* SIGURD]. Compose something? What do you think, Sigurd?

SIGURD. I think it is proper you should. You must do as she says.

DAGNY. Your neighbours in Iceland will think it wrong if there is no funeral song to sing when they drink to the memory of Örnulf's sons. There is always plenty of time to follow your sons.

ÖRNULF. Well, I shall try. And you listen, Dagny, so that you can record it later in runes!

[*The men come forward to form a group round him, with torches in their hands. He is silent for a short while, thinking, then he speaks.*]

> Hearts oppressed with sadness
> find no joy in singing;
> anguish racks the poet
> singing of his sorrow.
>
> God of song, who gave me
> precious gifts of language,
> hear my lamentation,
> mourn my loss so grievous.
>
> [*Rises.*]
>
> Cruel Fate has harshly
> ravaged my career,
> stolen joy and laughter,
> stricken Örnulf's treasure.
>
> Seven sons had Örnulf,
> by the great gods given—
> now alone he wanders,
> old and bent and sonless.

Seven sons, so handsome,
born and bred to sword-play,
formed a mighty bulwark
round the white-haired Viking.

Now the bulwark's broken,
now my sons lie lifeless;
joyless stands their father,
desolate his household.

Thorolf! Ah! my youngest!
resolute and dauntless!
stilled would be my sorrow
had but *you* survived them!

Fair you were, like springtime,
fond son of your father;
showing splendid promise
of a hero's future.

Tragic was his death-wound,
sore the pain inflicted,
crushed my heart within me
as by bands of iron.

Jealous Fate denied me
nothing of her vengeance,
strewed the path of Örnulf
deep with anguished heartache.

Feeble now my manhood;
were the gods to give me
strength, I'd want but one thing:
vengeance on this goddess.

One thing I would strive for:
her abrupt destruction . . .
she, who robbed and plundered
all I held most precious.

Has she taken all things!
No! I keep one asset!
still in my possession.
is the gift of poetry.

[*With rising enthusiasm.*]

Of my sons she stripped me,
yet the arts of language
still are mine, by which to
voice my grief in singing.

To my speech she granted
gifts of lyric power—
so my song shall echo
though my sons lie lifeless.

Hail, my sons courageous!
Hail, returning warriors!
thus the gift god-given
heals our grief and anguish!

[*He draws a deep breath, pushes his hair away from his face, and speaks calmly.*]

So! Örnulf is sound and strong again! [*To the men.*] Come along and have supper, lads. We have had a hard day's work!

[*He goes with the men into the boat-house.*]

DAGNY. Praise be to the gods in heaven for giving me this idea! [*To* SIGURD.] Won't you go in?

SIGURD. No, I don't much want to. Tell me, is everything ready for tomorrow?

DAGNY. It is. A silk-sewn shroud is lying on the bench inside. But I know that you will hold out against Gunnar, so I did not weep as I made it.

SIGURD. May the gods grant that you never have to weep for my sake.

[*He stops and looks out.*]

DAGNY. What are you listening for?

SIGURD. Don't you hear? . . . There!

[*He points to the left.*]

DAGNY. Yes . . . like a strange storm over the sea!

SIGURD [*going towards the background*]. H'm, it will hail hard in a storm like that. [*Shouts.*] Who goes there?

KAARE [*off stage, left*]. No stranger, Sigurd!

[KAARE *and a group of armed men enter from the left.*]

SIGURD. Where are you making for?

KAARE. For Gunnar's place!

SIGURD. To make trouble?

KAARE. Yes, for sure. You stopped me earlier. But I imagine you are quite glad to see it happen now!

SIGURD. That could be.

KAARE. I've heard about your dealings with Gunnar. But if I have *my* way, Gunnar will not altogether be terribly well equipped to meet you tomorrow.

SIGURD. This is a risky thing you are thinking of! You beware, Kaare!

KAARE [*with defiant laughter*]. Leave that to me. If you want to rig your ship tonight, we'll see you get plenty of light! Come on, men! Here's the path!

[*They all go out right, at the back.*]

DAGNY. Sigurd! Sigurd! You must stop this dreadful thing!

SIGURD [*crosses swiftly to the door, and shouts in*]. Up, Örnulf! Revenge on Kaare!

ÖRNULF [*comes out, with the rest*]. Kaare! Where is he?

SIGURD. He's making for Gunnar's house to set fire to it with everybody inside!

ÖRNULF. Ha! Let him! That will give me revenge on Gunnar and Hjördis now. Then I can deal with Kaare later.

SIGURD. No, there's little point in that. If you want to get Kaare, you must find him tonight. Because once this foul thing is done, he will make for the mountains. Gunnar I have challenged to a duel—you can be sure of him, even if I myself. . . . Well, no matter. . . . Tonight he must be protected from his enemies. It would be a bad thing if I were deprived of my revenge by a miserable wretch like Kaare!

ÖRNULF. It is true what you say. Though he killed Thorolf, I will protect him tonight. But tomorrow he must die!

SIGURD. He or I—of that you can be certain.

ÖRNULF. Come, then, and revenge Örnulf's sons!

[*He goes out with the men to the right, back.*]

SIGURD. Go with them, Dagny. I must stay here. For the news of our duel has already reached people, and I must not meet Gunnar before the proper time. But you . . . you go and advise your father. He must act with honour. There are many women on Gunnar's estate; no harm must come to Hjördis or any of the others.

DAGNY. Yes, yes, I'll go. And thank you for thinking of Hjördis like this!

SIGURD. Go, go, Dagny!

DAGNY. I am going. But we need not worry about Hjördis. She has a suit of shining gilt armour in her room, and she'll take care of herself.

SIGURD. That's what I think, too. But do go, all the same, and guide your father. Watch over them all and . . . over Gunnar's wife!

DAGNY. Trust me! We meet again soon!

[*She goes after the others.*]

SIGURD. This is the first time I stand weaponless while my blood-brother is in danger. [*Listens.*] I can hear shouts and the noise of swords . . . they are already there! [*Begins to walk over to the right, but stops and falls back in astonishment.*] Hjördis! She's coming here!

[HJÖRDIS *enters, dressed in a short, crimson kirtle, with gilt armour— helmet, breastplate, arm and leg pieces. Her hair is flying loose. On her back, she wears a quiver and at her belt a small shield. In her hand she carries the bow with the bow-string of her own hair. She comes in hurriedly, looking behind her as if afraid of something following her. She goes up close to* SIGURD, *seizes his arm, and speaks in a low voice.*]

HJÖRDIS. Sigurd! Sigurd! Can you see it?

SIGURD. What? Where?

HJÖRDIS. The wolf . . . *there*. Just behind me. It does not move. It glares at me with its two red eyes! . . . It is my death phantom, Sigurd! Three times it has appeared to me. That means that I must die tonight!

SIGURD. Hjördis! Hjördis!

HJÖRDIS. There it sinks into the ground! Ah, it has given its warning.

SIGURD. You are sick! Come in here!

HJÖRDIS. No, I shall wait here. I haven't much time left!

SIGURD. What has happened to you?

HJÖRDIS. Happened to me? I don't know. But it was true what you said today about Dagny and Gunnar standing between us. We must get away from them, and from this life. Then we can be together!

SIGURD. We . . . ? Ah, you mean . . . !

HJÖRDIS [*with dignity*]. I became homeless in this world the day you made another woman your wife. That was not well done! A man can give all things to his faithful friend . . . everything except the woman he loves. For if he does that, he breaks the secret web of Fate, and two lives are wrecked. A voice within keeps saying I was meant to use my inner strength to cheer and sustain you when times were hard; and that you were born as the one man in whom I could find all those things I felt were great and noble. For this I know, Sigurd—had we two held together, you would have been the most famous of men, and I the happiest of women.

SIGURD. These regrets serve no purpose now. Do you think there is any happiness in the life that awaits me now? Living day after day with Dagny, and shamming a love that chokes my heart. And yet it must be. It cannot be altered.

HJÖRDIS [*in a growing frenzy*]. It *must* be! We must both quit this life! You see this bow-string? With that I cannot miss, because I have sat over it singing incantations! [*She places an arrow in the bow, which is tensed.*] Listen! Listen to the rush of the wind! That is the dead, making their last journey. My spells brought them here . . . we shall join their company.

SIGURD [*steps back*]. Hjördis! Hjördis! You frighten me!

HJÖRDIS [*without heeding him*]. No power can alter our fate now! Ah, yes . . . and it is better so than if you had married me here in this life . . . than if I had sat in your house weaving linen and wool and bearing your children . . . pah!

SIGURD. Stop! Your witchcraft has been too much for you. It has left you sick in mind! [*In horror.*] Ha! Look! Gunnar's house . . . it is on fire!

HJÖRDIS. Let it burn! Let it burn! The mansion up in the clouds is better than any timber house of Gunnar's!

SIGURD. But Egil, your son . . . ! They will kill him!

HJÖRDIS. Let him die . . . then my shame will die with him.

SIGURD. And Gunnar . . . they will take your husband's life!

HJÖRDIS. What do I care! I shall go home with a better husband to-night! Yes, Sigurd! It must be so! This place holds no happiness for me. . . . The White God makes for the north. I do not wish to meet him. The old gods are no longer strong, not as they were before. . . . They sleep, they are almost like shades. . . . We shall fight them! Out of this life, Sigurd! I will set you on the throne of heaven, and I will sit by your side! [*The storm rages.*] Listen! Listen! There is our escort! Can you see the black horses racing by? One for me and one for you. . . . [*She raises her bow and shoots.*] Away, then, on your last journey!

SIGURD. Well aimed, Hjördis!

[*He falls.*]

HJÖRDIS [*joyfully, as she rushes across to him*]. Sigurd! My brother! . . . Now we belong together!

SIGURD. Less now than ever. This is the parting of our ways. For I am a Christian.

HJÖRDIS [*aghast*]. You . . . ! Ah, no! No!

SIGURD. The White God is mine. King Æthelstan taught me to know him. . . . It is to him I go now.

HJÖRDIS [*in despair*]. And I . . . ! [*Drops her bow.*] Alas! alas!

SIGURD. My life has been heavy ever since the moment I took you out of my own heart and gave you to Gunnar. Thank you, Hjördis! . . . Now I am so light and free.

[*He dies.*]

HJÖRDIS [*quietly*]. Dead! Then mine is indeed a wasted soul! [*The storm increases and she cries out wildly.*] They are coming! My spells bring them here! No, no! I will not come with you! I will not ride without Sigurd! No good . . . they can see me! They are laughing, they are waving to me! They spur on their horses! [*She rushes to the edge of the cliff in the background.*] Here they are upon me . . . and nowhere to shelter, nowhere to hide! Yes, perhaps at the bottom of the sea!

[*She throws herself over. One by one,* ÖRNULF, DAGNY, GUNNAR *and* EGIL, *together with* SIGURD's *and* ÖRNULF's MEN *come in from the right.*]

ÖRNULF [*turned to the gravemound*]. Now you can sleep in peace. You are not left unavenged!

DAGNY [*entering*]. Father! Father! I am nearly dead with terror. . . . All those bloody deeds . . . and the storm. . . . Listen! Listen!

GUNNAR [*with* EGIL *in his arms*]. Peace, and shelter for my child!

ÖRNULF. Gunnar!

GUNNAR. Yes, Örnulf! My house is burnt and my men are dead. I am in your power. Do what you will!

ÖRNULF. That rests with Sigurd. But come in under this roof. It is not safe out here!

DAGNY. Yes, in! [*She goes over to the boat-house, catches sight of the body and lets out a shriek.*] Sigurd, my husband! . . . They have killed him!

[*She throws herself down beside him.*]

ÖRNULF [*hurrying up*]. Sigurd!

GUNNAR [*putting* EGIL *down*]. Sigurd killed!

DAGNY [*looks wild-eyed at the men standing round the body*]. No, no, it cannot be! . . . He must still be alive! [*Sees the bow.*] Ha! What is this!

[*She gets up.*]

ÖRNULF. It is as you first said, my daughter. . . . Sigurd has been killed.

GUNNAR [*as if seized by a sudden thought*]. And Hjördis! Has Hjördis been here?

DAGNY [*quietly and controlled*]. I do not know. But this I do know: her bow has been here.

GUNNAR. Ah! As I thought!

DAGNY. Hush! [*To herself.*] How bitterly she must have hated him!

GUNNAR [*softly*]. Killed him . . . the night before our duel. She must still have loved me, then.

[*They all start back in terror, as they hear the sound of 'Aasgaards-rejden' in the air—the last ride of the dead on their way to Valhalla.*]

EGIL [*in terror*]. Father! Look!

GUNNAR. What is it?

EGIL. Up there . . . all those black horses . . . !

GUNNAR. It is only the clouds. . . .

ÖRNULF. No, it is the last ride of the dead.

EGIL [*with a shriek*]. Mother is with them!

DAGNY. Merciful powers!

GUNNAR. What are you saying, child!

EGIL. There . . . in front . . . on the black horse! Father! Father!

[EGIL *clings in terror to his father. A short pause. The storm passes, the clouds part, and the moon shines serenely over the landscape.*]

GUNNAR [*quietly and sadly*]. Now Hjördis is surely dead!

ÖRNULF. That is probably so, Gunnar . . . and on her I had more to avenge than on you. This meeting has cost us both dear. . . . There is my hand! Let us make peace!

GUNNAR. Thank you, Örnulf! And now aboard. I am sailing with you to Iceland!

ÖRNULF. Yes, to Iceland! This journey will not be easily forgotten:

> Sing of these heroic battles,
> mighty deeds on Norway's strand,
> down through Iceland's generations
> thrilling every Northern land.

Printed in Great Britain by
The Camelot Press Ltd., London and Southampton